LAMB'S CRITICISM

A SELECTION FROM THE LITERARY CRITICISM
OF CHARLES LAMB, EDITED WITH AN INTRO-
DUCTION AND SHORT NOTES BY

E. M. W. TILLYARD
M.A., O.B.E.
LATE FELLOW OF JESUS COLLEGE

GREENWOOD PRESS, PUBLISHERS
WESTPORT, CONNECTICUT

Originally published in 1923
by Cambridge University Press

Reprinted from an original copy in the collections
of the Brooklyn Public Library

First Greenwood Reprinting 1970

Library of Congress Catalogue Card Number 77-95108

SBN 8371-3121-9

Printed in the United States of America

PREFACE

THE literary criticism of Charles Lamb, scattered as it is through *The Essays of Elia*, the miscellaneous prose writings and the letters, is perhaps less easy to get at than that of any other great English critic. I venture, therefore, to hope that the collection of the best of it into a small volume may prove useful.

The following pieces have been included in their entirety: *Stage Illusion, Sanity of True Genius, Some Sonnets of Sir Philip Sydney, Dramatic Writers Contemporary with Shakspeare, On the Tragedies of Shakspeare, On the Poetical Works of George Wither, The Genteel Style in Writing, Estimate of De Foe's Secondary Novels*, the Review of Wordsworth's *Excursion*, the Review of Keats' *Lamia*.

The dates appended to the extracts from the letters refer to the date of writing, those appended to the other extracts refer to the date of first publication.

My thanks are due: to Mr Humphrey Milford for his generous permission to use the text of the Oxford Edition of the works of Charles and Mary Lamb; to Messrs J. M. Dent and Sons for permission to use the text of the Everyman Edition of Lamb's letters for most of my extracts from the letters; to Messrs Macmillan and Co. for permission to use the extracts from the letters of Lamb to the Lloyds; to Mr E. V. Lucas for kindly allowing me to include the review of Keats' *Lamia*, so happily recovered by him from the pages of *The New Times*; and to Sir Ambrose Elton for permission to include extracts from a letter of Lamb to Sir C. A. Elton.

E. M. W. T.

April 1923.

CONTENTS

CONTENTS

INTRODUCTION

1. LAMB AS A LITERARY CRITIC

THE position a man will give to Charles Lamb as a literary critic depends on what he believes the highest criticism to be. Does he seek information or enlightenment of it? should it persuade him by argument or like the Sublime of Longinus transport him by its power? For if he goes to it chiefly for facts, for arguments, for masterly comparisons, for sustained intellectual effort, he will find Lamb deficient, disagreeing probably with several of Lamb's contentions and condemning his critical writings as occasional, unmethodical and fragmentary; but if he goes to it for something that by some subtle means brings him closer to certain works of art than he has been able to get unaided, for something that creates in his mind the right receptive mood, then he will put Lamb among the very greatest of critics.

One may, without any disparagement of the criticism which informs, conclude that the criticism which transports is the higher kind, because it is rather artistic than intellectual, depending more than the other on the form it takes, for the full expression of its meaning. It is, in fact, the kind that it is now the fashion to call creative. But there is far more danger inherent in the creative than in the everyday kind; not when the result is inartistic, for then the failure is obvious, but when the critic reads himself into the author he studies and under the guise of criticism gives you an artistic expression of what are predominantly his own emotions. Then, the very beauty of the production endangers critical truth, just as to Plato the very beauty of all poetry was like a Siren-song that diverted men's minds from the proper philosophic serenity. The obvious example in English of creative criticism gone wrong is Francis Thompson's *Essay on Shelley*, where the author's slightly morbid feelings about childhood impair his vision, and impel him to exaggerate the little childishnesses and tricksinesses, which though charming should not be allowed to obscure the fundamental strength of Shelley's character, and where the beautiful exuberance of fancy and language is only too apt to make one think that they tell the truth not only about Francis Thompson (which they *do*) but about Shelley likewise. Thus it is that a man may well prefer the safer and less ambitious forms of criticism, in which reason is mixed in larger proportion, and caprice has less chance to do mischief; but yet it must be admitted that the highest successes in criticism are only possible when the greatest measure of emotion enters in and the consequent risks of falsehood are the greatest.

The greatest, like any other, criticism may be either theoretical or applied. It may be something (like Coleridge's 'willing suspension of disbelief that constitutes the moment of poetic faith') that illumines the working of the poetic process or of the aesthetic sense, or it may be, like Sainte-Beuve's essay on Cowper, something that recreates the critic's impression in a separate work of art, which, whether by a greater simplicity than existed in the original creation or by a slight exaggeration of what is peculiar or unique, leads the reader to a more intimate understanding of the original than would have been possible without its help. Of English masters of theoretical criticism Coleridge is the greatest, of applied, in a sense, Lamb.

To exalt Lamb so high may seem rash in view of the comparatively small bulk of his work and of his being so obviously an amateur, not, like Hazlitt, a professional critic; and if one were to judge Lamb as any kind of critic other than the creative, the claim would be preposterous. But the fact is that the bulk of criticism that is both a high work of art in itself and tells the truth about what it deals with is remarkably small and correspondingly precious. This should not be in the least surprising, if we consider the qualities that must go to the making of a great critic of authors. He must have the mind of a poet, a cool head, the faculty of self-surrender and a certain modicum of bookishness; probably many other qualities, but these will suffice. Some great men who have the qualification of being poets entirely lack at least one of the other necessary qualities. Great egotists like Milton and Wordsworth could never surrender their personalities in reading another author; Swinburne and Francis Thompson, even at their best, cannot keep cool enough to give that impression of ultimate conviction that the greatest criticism must give; Byron and Wordsworth had not the necessary bookishness. I doubt even if Coleridge has the quality of self-surrender sufficiently to make his criticism of authors supreme: his greatness lies rather in his many brilliant aphorisms on literary theory. The list of the greatest critics of authors is bound to be small; and I believe that if some inspired person were to collect all the quintessential criticism of authors that exists in English, Lamb's might well figure the most largely in that slender anthology.

I may be able to make my plea for Lamb's high position appear more reasonable, if I illustrate what I mean by quintessential criticism. Dryden's eulogy of Shakespeare in *The Essay of Dramatic Poesy* is admittedly fine: its justice, gusto and eloquence cannot be doubted; it is memorable as the first sustained appreciation of Shakespeare; Dryden shows in it a splendid independence of judgment. Many reasons contribute to making it precious, but still, to my thinking, it is at least one degree remoter than certain other pieces of criticism from the centre of truth. Sidney is in general a much smaller critic than Dryden, but twice at least he has penetrated nearer the truth than Dryden ever did: once when in comparing the world of nature with the poet's he fixes in words 'the breath and finer spirit' of romance, and again when he speaks of the *Ballad of Chevy Chase*. The difference between Sidney's criticism of *Chevy Chase* and Dryden's of Shakespeare is that the one is quite, the other not quite indispensable to what it criticises. We should be sorry to lose Dryden's eulogy of Shakespeare, but without it we should not appreciate Shakespeare the less, whereas Sidney's phrase, like a reflector in a lamp, permanently increases the value of ballad literature, is indeed almost a part of it, and if lost would carry away not a little of its virtue.

Now it is the first and greatest glory of Lamb's criticism that not a little of it has got just this quality of indispensableness. The *Lear* passage has grown to be almost inseparable from the play: we simply cannot do without the 'smatch of Tartarus and the souls in bale' and the rest of that great passage to enrich our appreciation of *The Duchess of Malfi*. Nor is this quality confined to a few famous places: it meets us again and again. Take a single sentence about Sidney's exuberant language: 'The images which lie before our feet (though by some accounted the only natural) are least natural for the high Sydnean love to express its fancies by.' This I consider indispensable criticism of Sidney, something quite irreplaceable. If asked for my reasons I could only say that the sentence, 'Sidney did not find a homely poetic imagery the most natural for expressing the kind of passion he felt,' although giving the same 'thought' as Lamb's sentence, is not in the least indispensable, or quote Professor Saintsbury to the effect that 'in no critic perhaps—not even in Mr Pater—does style count for so much as in Lamb.' To call attention to other indispensable passages should be unnecessary, when they are at hand in the text of this book.

But if it is impossible to analyse the essence of Lamb's most memorable passages, there is one obvious contributory reason why he succeeded in penetrating so near the centre of truth; namely that his very faults, his amateurishness and lack of range, helped him to concentrate the more intensely on what he loved, and to reach a more intimate sympathy with it. There are men, of whom Dryden and Hazlitt are conspicuous among the English, who react with vitality to almost any good literature that they meet, men with quick initial perceptions and strong immediate judgments. Their very versatility prevents quite that close intimacy which is such a peculiar property of Lamb. Not that they are open to the charge of superficiality, but that they have not the faculty of brooding over what they read as Lamb had. You feel that in them there is always present the desire to express in words what they feel about the books they read, and that they are always a little restless until they have expressed themselves. But when Lamb is 'hanging over (for the thousandth time) some passage in old Burton, or one of his strange contemporaries,' his mood is one of unspoiled serenity, and the waters of his spirit receive the perfect reflection of what he reads, unstirred by any wind of restlessness.

It is very easy to exaggerate the 'quaintness' of Lamb's writings in general, and it is positively wrong to use the word as peculiarly descriptive of his criticism. Nobility and high seriousness are terms that can more fittingly be applied to his greatest, modesty and simplicity to his lesser, and originality to all his criticism. There is nobility, high seriousness and a passionate emphasis in the essay *On the Tragedies of Shakspeare* and even in the mutilated review of *The Excursion*. Moreover Lamb's fundamental concern was with the literature of human action rather than of fancy, and could not have co-existed with a fundamental quaintness. 'The plays which I made choice of,' he writes at the beginning of the *Characters of Dramatic Writers, Contemporary with Shakspeare*, 'were, with few exceptions, such as treat of human life and manners, rather than masques and Arcadian pastorals, with their train of abstractions, unimpassioned deities, passionate mortals—Claius, and Medorus, and Amintas, and Amarillis. My leading design was, to illustrate what may be called the moral sense of our ancestors.' These are not the words of one whose quaintness is fundamental: the spirit in which they are written would not have been disowned by Matthew Arnold. This concern with human action is nowhere better seen than in the admirable review of Keats' *Lamia* volume, in which Lamb with an instinct perfectly true to himself, though not necessarily truer than the instincts of those who have thought otherwise, prefers *Isabella* with its greater insistence on action, human feeling and dramatic qualities generally to all the splendour of the pictorial writing in *The Eve of St Agnes*. He could never have shown this preference, had his critical turn of mind been above all things quaint.

Lamb's modesty and simplicity (so beautifully described in Pater's essay in *Appreciations*) are evident with the rarest exceptions throughout his letters, from his earliest criticisms of Coleridge to his latest of Moxon. He never tries to be clever; he never in the slightest degree lords it over those who have delivered themselves into his hand by showing him their works. What he criticises and how he can help it are everything, his own glory as critic nothing. The same qualities are to be found in the passage on Sir William Temple in *The Genteel Style in Writing*. I can imagine no more perfect introduction to a writer than this. Lamb works here largely by quotation, but every now and then delicately adjusts the reader's mood by a judicious remark. At the end we have forgotten the critic, and are left with an inexplicably vivid impression of Temple and a vehement desire to learn all there is to know about him. How many a modern review do we read with the feeling that the reviewer is a very clever fellow, but that we are not particularly drawn to learn more of his subject! Professor Elton excellently expresses this impersonality of Lamb's criticism in a brief comparison of Lamb and Hazlitt. 'Hazlitt's zest and connoisseurship are equally keen, but he has something less than Lamb's re-creative power, and he identifies himself less with the thing he loves, though he loves it as much. He communicates his own enjoyment, and makes us a defiant present of it, as *his*; but in Lamb the old poet speaks again, as though his spirit were but taking up a new instrument and breathing through it.'

Of Lamb's originality it is superfluous to speak: it meets us everywhere in the good and the bad alike. He had no master, his tastes were entirely native, and there is hardly a line of his criticism that anyone else could have written.

Lamb's defects as a critic were frankly implied by himself in more than one confessional passage, roundly stated by Hazlitt, admitted by De Quincey, and they have been duly recorded in the great modern *History of Criticism*.

Lamb confesses in *Imperfect Sympathies* that his mind is desultory, sadly lacking in system, 'suggestive merely' and 'content with fragments and scattered pieces of Truth.' Granted that he was true enough to his nature to make out the worst case he could against himself, we must admit that his self-accusation is substantially true. It is impossible to deny that Lamb was lacking in range, that his attainments as a scholar were not great, that his knowledge of foreign literature depended mostly on translations and even so was not wide, that he read what he liked, not what he ought, and so on. But is lack of range such a very serious fault? Cannot the virtue of immense reading be exaggerated? The total amount of great literature extant in the world is very large. A few supermen, uniting a high vitality with powerful eyesight, prodigious memories, a highly developed patience of sitting in chairs and a small desire for sleep, may gain more than a superficial acquaintance with most of it, and retain their faculty for appreciation. But I cannot believe that such range is desirable except for a few, or that those few can have the intensity of appreciation of a Lamb. Those who exact vast range in a critic underestimate the expenditure of emotional force that must go to a great appreciation of a masterpiece. It is futile to expect any one man to enjoy the accumulated outpourings of the great minds of many ages in any worthy degree of intensity.

Then there is the charge brought by Hazlitt in his essay *On Criticism* in *Table Talk* that Lamb has an invincible predilection for the obscure, and cannot appreciate anything that appeals to the multitude. That Lamb was attracted by the curious and the out-of-the-way, and that he liked to feel that he was appreciating something neglected by others or appreciating in an unusual way something known, cannot be denied.

It was a pleasure to him to appreciate Wither, the luckless butt of ignorant Augustan abuse, and he gets peculiar pleasure in saying in his essay on him, 'Whoever expects to find in the satirical pieces of this writer any of those peculiarities which pleased him in the satires of Dryden or Pope, will be grievously disappointed.' He has in fact got very strongly the antiquarian delight of collecting rarities. Yet this delight is not fundamental, but an added zest. Primarily he seeks what he likes; if what he likes happens to be rare, if he can work his way through a little dust to some neglected piece of human passion, so much the better; but he does not allow mere antiquarianism to affect his tastes. He is, as it were, a man who in 1860 admires Chippendale chairs, not an original who in 1923 deliberately adorns his house with the furniture of 1860: even in 1923 he would have liked Chippendale chairs, though with just a trifle less relish. It is as wrong to consider Lamb's occultism and antiquarianism as his most important characteristics as it is to exaggerate his quaintness. His chief concern was with great literature, in particular with Shakespeare, but when, to use the phrase of literary appreciation, he took 'an airing beyond the diocese of the strict conscience' (and who can live for very long at a stretch in the rarefied atmosphere of the great masterpieces?) his antiquarian instincts asserted themselves. 'And yet,' says Pater in his essay on Lamb, 'delicate, refining, daintily epicurean, as he may seem, when he writes of giants, such as Hogarth or Shakespeare, though often but in a stray note, you catch the sense of veneration with which those great names in past literature and art brooded over his intelligence, his undiminished impressibility by the great effects in them.'

Then there is Hazlitt's other charge, of fickleness, in a famous passage in *A Farewell to Essay Writing* proclaiming his own consistency. 'Even Lamb, whose relish of certain things is as keen and earnest as possible, takes a surfeit of admiration, and I should be afraid to ask about his select authors or particular friends, after a lapse of ten years.' That Lamb's tastes and judgments developed as he grew up is undeniable. For instance, writing to Coleridge in 1796, he puts Beaumont and Fletcher and then Massinger in merit next to Shakespeare, a judgment not maintained in the notes to the *Specimens* in 1808. But can a man be blamed if his judgments are not fully formed by the age of twenty-one, Lamb's age when he wrote to Coleridge in 1796? Apart from this natural growth it would be natural enough, inevitable perhaps, that Lamb's concentrated appreciation should result now and then in a surfeit: but is there any evidence of a serious change of allegiance? It is just conceivable that once or twice in his life he may have lost his taste for the *Religio Medici*, as one human being may turn for a moment from another he loves exceedingly; but is there the least thing to suggest that he ever turned against it for good?

But I have spent quite enough words in palliating Lamb's defects, for, when all is said and done, they are quite innocuous. He made mistakes: he admired Southey overmuch; he spoke contemptuously of *Faust*; he did not give Shelley a chance. But his mistakes are not such as mislead; sheep and goats in his criticism require no divine aid in the separation. If he states one side of a question only, as in the essay on *Shakspeare's Tragedies* and *The Artificial Comedy of the Last Century*, he in no way makes us forget that there is another side, and withal gives us high criticism that entirely transcends the nominal issue. His native frankness and sincerity keep his most questionable assertions from being in the least more dangerous than Dr Johnson's enchanting strictures on *Lycidas*.

2. METHOD OF SELECTING

To say that in selecting passages from Lamb's literary criticism I have confined myself to what is literary and what is critical may seem unnecessary: nevertheless I wish to make it clear that I have set myself these limits. I have excluded the essay *On the Genius and Character of Hogarth*, which for all its excellence cannot be called literary. I have also excluded some very interesting passages about literature which I cannot call critical in any high sense of the word. Among these is the *Detached Thoughts on Books and Reading*, which talks charmingly round the books rather than gets inside them; the passage about Blake in a letter to Barton of May 15, 1824, which for all its interest mainly tells us what Lamb has not read and that 'Tiger, Tiger' is glorious; and the brief mention of *Rose Aylmer* in a letter to Landor of April 9, 1832, which is interesting in recounting that the poem had for Lamb an inexplicable charm, but critically disappointing because it does not convey to us any hint of the nature of that charm. I have likewise excluded a number of short passages and phrases which in my judgment just fall short of true criticism. I can make clear my limiting line by a couple of examples. I have included in my text the single phrase, 'The beautiful obliquities of the Religio Medici,' a phrase which by subtle workings of rhythm and word-combinations distils for us the very essence of the book it names. On the other hand, when Lamb adjures Coleridge to attempt an epic 'by the dainty, sweet, and soothing phantasies of honey-tongued Spenser,' I feel he is not being critical. The phrase charms us by its Elizabethan echoes, but tells us nothing about Spenser we do not know already: I have not included it. The first sentence as it were makes a spark, the second does not. It is my hope that each extract I have chosen contains at least one spark!

Lamb's criticism, often working delicately and indirectly, must in its nature appeal so differently to different people, that I have not the smallest expectation that this selection will satisfy all or the majority of the lovers of Lamb who may chance to see it. Every Elian, I feel sure, will be scandalised at the omission of one or more of his favourite passages, which unluckily did not appeal so strongly to me.

I have confined myself entirely to what I consider good criticism, except for the passages concerning Goethe, Byron and Shelley, which are added to illustrate Lamb's defects.

After hesitation I have included the review of *The Excursion*. I should say that the ghost of Lamb strongly resents its preservation, but for *that* the editors of Lamb's collected works are responsible; and even in its mutilated state we cannot really do without it.

As far as possible I have classified extracts by authors or groups of authors. The two that could not be thus classed I have left under their own titles. I have arranged the authors almost always in the chronological sequence of their births.

LAMB'S LITERARY CRITICISM

STAGE ILLUSION

A play is said to be well or ill acted in proportion to the scenical illusion produced. Whether such illusion can in any case be perfect, is not the question. The nearest approach to it, we are told, is, when the actor appears wholly unconscious of the presence of spectators. In tragedy—in all which is to affect the feelings—this undivided attention to his stage business, seems indispensable. Yet it is, in fact, dispensed with every day by our cleverest tragedians; and while these references to an audience, in the shape of rant or sentiment, are not too frequent or palpable, a sufficient quantity of illusion for the purposes of dramatic interest may be said to be produced in spite of them. But, tragedy apart, it may be inquired whether, in certain characters in comedy, especially those which are a little extravagant, or which involve some notion repugnant to the moral sense, it is not a proof of the highest skill in the comedian when, without absolutely appealing to an audience, he keeps up a tacit understanding with them; and makes them, unconsciously to themselves, a party in the scene. The utmost nicety is required in the mode of doing this; but we speak only of the great artists in the profession.

The most mortifying infirmity in human nature, to feel in ourselves, or to contemplate in another, is, perhaps, cowardice. To see a coward *done to the life* upon a stage would produce anything but mirth. Yet we most of us remember Jack Bannister's cowards. Could any thing be more agreeable, more pleasant? We loved the rogues. How was this effected but by the exquisite art of the actor in a perpetual sub-insinuation to us, the spectators, even in the extremity of the shaking fit, that he was not half such a coward as we took him for? We saw all the common symptoms of the malady upon him; the quivering lip, the cowering knees, the teeth chattering; and could have sworn 'that man was frightened.' But we forgot all the while—or kept it almost a secret to ourselves—that he never once lost his self-possession; that he let out by a thousand droll looks and gestures—meant at *us*, and not at all supposed to be visible to his fellows in the scene, that his confidence in his own resources had never once deserted him. Was this a genuine picture of a coward? or not rather a likeness, which the clever artist contrived to palm upon us instead of an original; while we secretly connived at the delusion for the purpose of greater pleasure, than a more genuine counterfeiting of the imbecility, helplessness, and utter self-desertion, which we know to be concomitants of cowardice in real life, could have given us?

Why are misers so hateful in the world, and so endurable on the stage, but because the skilful actor, by a sort of subreference, rather than direct appeal to us, disarms the character of a great deal of its odiousness, by seeming to engage *our* compassion for the insecure tenure by which he holds his money bags and parchments? By this subtle vent half of the hatefulness of the character—the self-closeness with which in real life it coils itself up from the sympathies of men—evaporates. The miser becomes sympathetic; *i.e.* is no genuine miser. Here again a diverting likeness is substituted for a very disagreeable reality.

Spleen, irritability—the pitiable infirmities of old men, which produce only pain to behold in the realities, counterfeited upon a stage, divert not altogether for the comic appendages to them, but in part from an inner conviction that they are *being acted* before us; that a likeness only is going on, and not the thing itself. They please by being done under the life, or beside it; not *to the life*. When Gatty acts an old man, is he angry indeed? or only a pleasant counterfeit, just enough of a likeness to recognise, without pressing upon us the uneasy sense of reality?

Comedians, paradoxical as it may seem, may be too natural. It was the case with a late actor. Nothing could be more earnest or true than the manner of Mr Emery; this told excellently in his Tyke, and characters of a tragic cast. But when he carried the same rigid exclusiveness of attention to the stage business, and wilful blindness and oblivion of everything before the curtain into his comedy, it produced a harsh and dissonant effect. He was out of keeping with the rest of the *Personæ Dramatis*. There was as little link between him and them as betwixt himself and the audience. He was a third estate, dry, repulsive, and unsocial to all. Individually considered, his execution was masterly. But comedy is not this unbending thing; for this reason, that the same degree of credibility is not required of it as to serious scenes. The degrees of credibility demanded to the two things may be illustrated by the different sort of truth which we expect when a man tells us a mournful or a merry story. If we suspect the former of falsehood in any one tittle, we reject it altogether. Our tears refuse to flow at a suspected imposition. But the teller of a mirthful tale has latitude allowed him. We are content with less than absolute truth. 'Tis the same with dramatic illusion. We confess we love in comedy to see an audience naturalised behind the scenes, taken in into the interest of the drama, welcomed as by-standers however. There is something ungracious in a comic actor holding himself aloof from all participation or concern with those who are come to be diverted by him. Macbeth must see the dagger, and no ear but his own be told of it; but an old fool in farce may think he *sees something*, and by conscious words and looks express it, as plainly as he can speak, to pit, box, and gallery. When an impertinent in tragedy, an Osric, for instance, breaks in upon the serious passions of the scene, we approve of the contempt with which he is treated. But when the pleasant impertinent of comedy, in a piece purely meant to give delight, and raise mirth out of whimsical perplexities, worries the studious man with taking up his leisure, or making his house his home, the same sort of contempt expressed (however *natural*) would destroy the balance of delight in the spectators. To make the intrusion comic, the actor who plays the annoyed man must a little desert nature; he must, in short, be thinking of the audience, and express only so much dissatisfaction and peevishness as is consistent with the pleasure of comedy. In other words, his perplexity must seem half put on. If he repel the intruder with the sober set face of a man in earnest, and more especially if he deliver his expostulations in a tone which in the world must necessarily provoke a duel; his real-life manner will destroy the whimsical and purely dramatic existence of the other character (which to render it comic demands an antagonist comicality on the part of the character opposed to it), and convert what was meant for mirth, rather than belief, into a downright piece of impertinence indeed, which would raise no diversion in us, but rather stir pain, to see inflicted in earnest upon any worthy person. A very judicious actor (in most of his parts) seems to have fallen into an error of this sort in his playing with Mr Wrench in the farce of Free and Easy.

Many instances would be tedious; these may suffice to show that comic acting at least does not always demand from the performer that strict abstraction from all reference to an audience, which is exacted of it; but that in some cases a sort of compromise may take place, and all the purposes of dramatic delight be attained by a judicious understanding, not too openly announced, between the ladies and gentlemen—on both sides of the curtain.   *The Last Essays of Elia*. 1825.

SANITY OF TRUE GENIUS

So far from the position holding true, that great wit (or genius, in our modern way of speaking), has a necessary alliance with insanity, the greatest wits, on the contrary, will ever be found to be the sanest writers. It is impossible for the mind to conceive of a mad Shakspeare. The greatness of wit, by which the poetic talent is here chiefly to be understood, manifests itself in the admirable balance of all the faculties. Madness is the disproportionate straining or excess of any one of them. 'So strong a wit,' says Cowley, speaking of a poetical friend,

> ——did Nature to him frame,
> As all things but his judgment overcame,
> His judgment like the heavenly moon did show,
> Tempering that mighty sea below.

The ground of the mistake is, that men, finding in the raptures of the higher poetry a condition of exaltation, to which they have no parallel in their own experience, besides the spurious resemblance of it in dreams and fevers, impute a state of dreaminess and fever to the poet. But the true poet dreams being awake. He is not possessed by his subject, but has dominion over it. In the groves of Eden he walks familiar as in his native paths. He ascends the empyrean heaven, and is not intoxicated. He treads the burning marl without dismay; he wins his flight without self-loss through realms of chaos 'and old night.' Or if, abandoning himself to that severer chaos of a 'human mind untuned,' he is content awhile to be mad with Lear, or to hate mankind (a sort of madness) with Timon, neither is that madness, nor this misanthropy, so unchecked, but that,—never letting the reins of reason wholly go, while most he seems to do so,—he has his better genius still whispering at his ear, with the good servant Kent suggesting saner counsels, or with the honest steward Flavius recommending kindlier resolutions. Where he seems most to recede from humanity, he will be found the truest to it. From beyond the scope of Nature if he summon possible existences, he subjugates them to the law of her consistency. He is beautifully loyal to that sovereign directress, even when he appears most to betray and desert her. His ideal tribes submit to policy; his very monsters are tamed to his hand, even as that wild sea-brood, shepherded by Proteus. He tames, and he clothes them with attributes of flesh and blood, till they wonder at themselves, like Indian Islanders forced to submit to European vesture. Caliban, the Witches, are as true to the laws of their own nature (ours with a difference), as Othello, Hamlet, and Macbeth. Herein the great and the little wits are differenced; that if the latter wander ever so little from nature or actual existence, they lose themselves, and their readers. Their phantoms are lawless; their visions nightmares. They do not create, which implies shaping and consistency. Their imaginations are not active—for to be active is to call something into act and form—but passive, as men in sick dreams. For the super-natural, or something super-added to what we know of nature, they give you the plainly non-natural. And if this were all, and that these mental hallucinations were discoverable only in the treatment of subjects out of nature, or transcending it, the judgment might with some plea be pardoned if it ran riot, and a little wantonized: but even in the describing of real and every day life, that which is before their eyes, one of these lesser wits shall more deviate from nature—show more of that inconsequence, which has a natural alliance with frenzy, —than a great genius in his 'maddest fits,' as Withers somewhere calls them. We appeal to any one that is acquainted with the common run of Lane's novels,—as they existed some twenty or thirty years back,—those scanty intellectual viands of the whole female reading public, till a happier genius arose, and expelled for ever the innutritious phantoms,—whether he has not found his brain more 'betossed,' his memory more puzzled, his sense of when and where more confounded, among the improbable events, the incoherent incidents, the inconsistent characters, or no-characters, of some third-rate love intrigue—where the persons shall be a Lord Glendamour and a Miss Rivers, and the scene only alternate between Bath and

Bond-street—a more bewildering dreaminess induced upon him, than he has felt wandering over all the fairy grounds of Spenser. In the productions we refer to, nothing but names and places is familiar; the persons are neither of this world nor of any other conceivable one; an endless string of activities without purpose, of purposes destitute of motive:—we meet phantoms in our known walks; *fantasques* only christened. In the poet we have names which announce fiction; and we have absolutely no place at all, for the things and persons of the Fairy Queen prate not of their 'whereabout.' But in their inner nature, and the law of their speech and actions, we are at home and upon acquainted ground. The one turns life into a dream; the other to the wildest dreams gives the sobrieties of every day occurrences. By what subtile art of tracing the mental processes it is effected, we are not philosophers enough to explain, but in that wonderful episode of the cave of Mammon, in which the Money God appears first in the lowest form of a miser, is then a worker of metals, and becomes the god of all the treasures of the world; and has a daughter, Ambition, before whom all the world kneels for favours—with the Hesperian fruit, the waters of Tantalus, with Pilate washing his hands vainly, but not impertinently, in the same stream—that we should be at one moment in the cave of an old hoarder of treasures, at the next at the forge of the Cyclops, in a palace and yet in hell, all at once, with the shifting mutations of the most rambling dream, and our judgment yet all the time awake, and neither able nor willing to detect the fallacy,—is a proof of that hidden sanity which still guides the poet in his widest seeming-aberrations.

It is not enough to say that the whole episode is a copy of the mind's conceptions in sleep; it is, in some sort—but what a copy! Let the most romantic of us, that has been entertained all night with the spectacle of some wild and magnificent vision, recombine it in the morning, and try it by his waking judgment. That which appeared so shifting, and yet so coherent, while that faculty was passive, when it comes under cool examination, shall appear so reasonless and so unlinked, that we are ashamed to have been so deluded; and to have taken, though but in sleep, a monster for a god. But the transitions in this episode are every whit as violent as in the most extravagant dream, and yet the waking judgment ratifies them.

The Last Essays of Elia. 1826.

HESIOD

To read the *Days and Works* is like eating nice brown bread, homely sweet and nutritive.

Letter to C. A. Elton, Aug. 1824 (?).

SIR PHILIP SIDNEY

This way of description which seems unwilling ever to leave off, weaving parenthesis within parenthesis, was brought to its height by Sir Philip Sidney. He seems to have set the example to Shakspeare. Many beautiful instances may be found all over the Arcadia. These bountiful Wits always give full measure, pressed down, and running over.

Notes to Specimens of Dramatic Poets who lived about the Time of Shakspeare. 1808.

SOME SONNETS OF SIR PHILIP SYDNEY

Sydney's Sonnets—I speak of the best of them—are among the very best of their sort. They fall below the plain moral dignity, the sanctity, and high yet modest spirit of self-approval, of Milton, in his compositions of a similar structure. They are in truth what Milton, censuring the Arcadia, says of that work (to which they are a sort of after-tune or application), 'vain and amatorious' enough, yet the things in their kind (as he confesses to be true of the romance) may be 'full of worth and wit.' They savour of the Courtier, it must be allowed, and not of the Commonwealthsman. But Milton was a Courtier when he wrote the Masque at Ludlow Castle, and still more a Courtier when he composed the Arcades. When the national struggle was to begin, he becomingly cast these vanities behind him; and if the order of time had thrown Sir Philip upon the crisis which preceded the Revolution, there is no reason why he should not have acted the same part in that emergency, which has glorified the name of a later Sydney. He did not want for plainness or boldness of spirit. His letter on the French match may testify, he could speak his mind freely to Princes. The times did not call him to the scaffold.

The Sonnets which we oftenest call to mind of Milton were the compositions of his maturest years. Those of Sydney, which I am about to produce, were written in the very hey-day of his blood. They are stuck full of amorous fancies—far-fetched conceits, befitting his occupation; for True Love thinks no labour to send out Thoughts upon the vast, and more than Indian voyages, to bring home rich pearls, outlandish wealth, gums, jewels, spicery, to sacrifice in self-depreciating simili-tudes, as shadows of true amiabilities in the Beloved. We must be Lovers—or at least the cooling touch of time, the *circum præcordia frigus*, must not have so damped our faculties, as to take away our recollection that we were once so—before we can duly appreciate the glorious vanities, and graceful hyper-boles, of the passion. The images which lie before our feet (though by some accounted the only natural) are least natural for the high Sydnean love to express its fancies by. They may serve for the loves of Tibullus, or the dear Author of the Schoolmistress; for passions that creep and whine in Elegies and Pastoral Ballads. I am sure Milton never loved at this rate. I am afraid some of his addresses (*ad Leonoram* I mean) have rather erred on the farther side; and that the poet came not much short of a religious indecorum, when he could thus apostrophise a singing-girl:—

> Angelus unicuique suus (sic credite gentes)
>   Obtigit aetheriis ales ab ordinibus.
> Quid mirum, Leonora, tibi si gloria major,
>   Nam tua praesentem vox sonat ipsa Deum?
> Aut Deus, aut vacui certè mens tertia coeli,
>   Per tua secretô guttura serpit agens;
> Serpit agens, facilisque docet mortalia corda
>   Sensim immortali assuescere posse sono.
> QUOD SI CUNCTA QUIDEM DEUS EST, PER CUNCTAQUE FUSUS.
> IN TE UNÂ LOQUITUR, CAETERA MUTUS HABET.

This is loving in a strange fashion; and it requires some candour of construction (besides the slight darkening of a dead language) to cast a veil over the ugly appearance of some-thing very like blasphemy in the last two verses. I think the Lover would have been staggered, if he had gone about to express the same thought in English. I am sure, Sydney has no flights like this. His extravaganzas do not strike at the sky, though he takes leave to adopt the pale Dian into a fellowship with his mortal passions.

I

With how sad steps, O Moon, thou climb'st the skies;
How silently; and with how wan a face!
What! may it be, that even in heavenly place
That busy Archer his sharp arrows tries?
Sure, if that long-with-love-acquainted eyes
Can judge of love, thou feel'st a lover's case;
I read it in thy looks; thy languisht grace
To me, that feel the like, thy state descries.
Then, even of fellowship, O Moon, tell me,
Is constant love deem'd there but want of wit?
Are beauties there as proud as here they be?
Do they above love to be loved, and yet
Those lovers scorn, whom that love doth possess?
Do they call *virtue* there—*ungratefulness?*

The last line of this poem is a little obscured by transposition.
He means, Do they call ungratefulness there a virtue?

II

Come, Sleep, O Sleep, the certain knot of peace,
The baiting place of wit, the balm of woe,
The poor man's wealth, the prisoner's release,
The indifferent judge between the high and low;
With shield of proof shield me from out the prease[1]
Of those fierce darts despair at me doth throw;
O make in me those civil wars to cease:
I will good tribute pay, if thou do so.
Take thou of me sweet pillows, sweetest bed;
A chamber deaf to noise, and blind to light;
A rosy garland, and a weary head.
And if these things, as being thine by right,
Move not thy heavy grace, thou shalt in me,
Livelier than elsewhere, STELLA's image see.

III

The curious wits, seeing dull pensiveness
Bewray itself in my long-settled eyes,
Whence those same fumes of melancholy rise,
With idle pains, and missing aim, do guess.
Some, that know how my spring I did address,
Deem that my Muse some fruit of knowledge plies;
Others, because the Prince my service tries,
Think, that I think state errors to redress;
But harder judges judge, ambition's rage,
Scourge of itself, still climbing slippery place,
Holds my young brain captiv'd in golden cage.
O fools, or over-wise! alas, the race
Of all my thoughts hath neither stop nor start,
But only STELLA's eyes, and STELLA's heart.

[1] Press.

IV

Because I oft in dark abstracted guise
Seem most alone in greatest company,
With dearth of words, or answers quite awry,
To them that would make speech of speech arise;
They deem, and of their doom the rumour flies,
That poison foul of bubbling *Pride* doth lie
So in my swelling breast, that only I
Fawn on myself, and others do despise;
Yet *Pride*, I think, doth not my Soul possess,
Which looks too oft in his unflattering glass:
But one worse fault—*Ambition*—I confess,
That makes me oft my best friends overpass,
Unseen, unheard—while Thought to highest place
Bends all his powers, even unto STELLA'S grace.

V

Having this day, my horse, my hand, my lance,
Guided so well that I obtained the prize,
Both by the judgment of the English eyes,
And of some sent from that *sweet enemy*,—France;
Horsemen my skill in horsemanship advance;
Townsfolk my strength; a daintier judge applies
His praise to sleight, which from good use doth rise;
Some lucky wits impute it but to chance;
Others, because of both sides I do take
My blood from them, who did excel in this,
Think Nature me a man of arms did make.
How far they shot awry! the true cause is,
STELLA look'd on, and from her heavenly face
Sent forth the beams which made so fair my race.

VI

In martial sports I had my cunning tried,
And yet to break more staves did me address,
While with the people's shouts (I must confess)
Youth, luck, and praise, even fill'd my veins with pride
When Cupid, having me (his slave) descried
In Mars's livery, prancing in the press,
'What now, Sir Fool!' said he; 'I would no less:
Look here, I say.' I look'd, and STELLA spied,
Who hard by made a window send forth light.
My heart then quak'd, then dazzled were mine eyes;
One hand forgot to rule, th'other to fight;
Nor trumpet's sound I heard, nor friendly cries.
My foe came on, and beat the air for me—
Till that her blush made me my shame to see.

VII

No more, my dear, no more these counsels try;
O give my passions leave to run their race;
Let Fortune lay on me her worst disgrace;
Let folk o'er-charged with brain against me cry;
Let clouds bedim my face, break in mine eye;
Let me no steps, but of lost labour, trace;
Let all the earth with scorn recount my case—
But do not will me from my love to fly.
I do not envy Aristotle's wit,
Nor do aspire to Cæsar's bleeding fame;
Nor aught do care, though some above me sit;
Nor hope, nor wish, another course to frame,
But that which once may win thy cruel heart:
Thou art my wit, and thou my virtue art.

VIII

LOVE still a boy, and oft a wanton, is,
School'd only by his mother's tender eye;
What wonder then, if he his lesson miss,
When for so soft a rod dear play he try?
And yet my STAR, because a sugar'd kiss
In sport I suck'd, while she asleep did lie,
Doth lour, nay chide, nay threat, for only this.
Sweet, it was saucy LOVE, not humble I.
But no 'scuse serves; she makes her wrath appear
In beauty's throne—see now, who dares come near
Those scarlet judges, threat'ning bloody pain?
O heav'nly Fool, thy most kiss-worthy face
Anger invests with such a lovely grace,
That anger's self I needs must kiss again.

IX

I never drank of Aganippe well,
Nor ever did in shade of Tempe sit,
And Muses scorn with vulgar brains to dwell;
Poor lay-man I, for sacred rites unfit.
Some do I hear of Poets' fury tell,
But (God wot) wot not what they mean by it;
And this I swear by blackest brook of hell,
I am no pick-purse of another's wit.
How falls it then, that with so smooth an ease
My thoughts I speak, and what I speak doth flow
In verse, and that my verse best wits doth please?
Guess me the cause—what is it thus?—fye, no.
Or so?—much less. How then? sure thus it is,
My lips are sweet, inspired with STELLA's kiss.

X

Of all the kings that ever here did reign,
Edward, named Fourth, as first in praise I name,
Not for his fair outside, nor well-lined brain—
Although less gifts imp feathers oft on Fame.
Nor that he could, young-wise, wise-valiant, frame
His sire's revenge, join'd with a kingdom's gain;
And, gain'd by Mars could yet mad Mars so tame,
That Balance weigh'd what Sword did late obtain.
Nor that he made the Floure-de-luce so 'fraid,
Though strongly hedged of bloody Lions' paws
That witty Lewis to him a tribute paid.
Nor this, nor that, nor any such small cause—
But only, for this worthy knight durst prove
To lose his crown rather than fail his love.

XI

O happy Thames, that didst my STELLA bear,
I saw thyself, with many a smiling line
Upon thy cheerful face, Joy's livery wear,
While those fair planets on thy streams did shine;
The boat for joy could not to dance forbear,
While wanton winds, with beauty so divine
Ravish'd, stay'd not, till in her golden hair
They did themselves (O sweetest prison) twine.
And fain those Æol's youth there would their stay
Have made; but, forced by nature still to fly,
First did with puffing kiss those locks display.
She, so dishevell'd, blush'd; from window I
With sight thereof cried out, O fair disgrace,
Let honour's self to thee grant highest place!

XII

Highway, since you my chief Parnassus be;
And that my Muse, to some ears not unsweet,
Tempers her words to trampling horses' feet,
More soft than to a chamber melody,—
Now blessed You bear onward blessed Me
To Her, where I my heart safe left shall meet,
My Muse and I must you of duty greet
With thanks and wishes, wishing thankfully.
Be you still fair, honour'd by public heed,
By no encroachment wrong'd, nor time forgot;
Nor blam'd for blood, nor shamed for sinful deed.
And that you know, I envy you no lot
Of highest wish, I wish you so much bliss,
Hundreds of years you STELLA's feet may kiss.

Of the foregoing, the first, the second, and the last sonnet, are my favourites. But the general beauty of them all is, that they are so perfectly characteristical. The spirit of 'learning and of chivalry,'—of which union, Spenser has entitled Sydney to have been the 'president,'—shines through them. I confess I can see nothing of the 'jejune' or 'frigid' in them; much less of the 'stiff' and 'cumbrous'—which I have sometimes heard objected to the Arcadia. The verse runs off swiftly and gallantly. It might have been tuned to the trumpet; or tempered (as himself expresses it) to 'trampling horses' feet.' They abound in felicitous phrases—

> O heav'nly Fool, thy most kiss-worthy face—
>
> *8th Sonnet.*
>
> ————Sweet pillows, sweetest bed;
> A chamber deaf to noise, and blind to light;
> A rosy garland, and a weary head.
>
> *2nd Sonnet.*
>
> ————That sweet enemy,—France—
>
> *5th Sonnet.*

But they are not rich in words only, in vague and unlocalised feelings—the failing too much of some poetry of the present day—they are full, material, and circumstantiated. Time and place appropriates every one of them. It is not a fever of passion wasting itself upon a thin diet of dainty words, but a transcendent passion pervading and illuminating action, pursuits, studies, feats of arms, the opinions of contemporaries and his judgment of them. An historical thread runs through them, which almost affixes a date to them; marks the *when* and *where* they were written.

I have dwelt the longer upon what I conceive the merit of these poems, because I have been hurt by the wantonness (I wish I could treat it by a gentler name) with which W. H. takes every occasion of insulting the memory of Sir Philip Sydney. But the decisions of the Author of Table Talk, etc. (most profound and subtle where they are, as for the most part, just) are more safely to be relied upon, on subjects and authors he has a partiality for, than on such as he has conceived an accidental prejudice against. Milton wrote sonnets, and was a king-hater; and it was congenial perhaps to sacrifice a courtier to a patriot. But I was unwilling to lose a *fine idea* from my mind. The noble images, passions, sentiments, and poetical delicacies of character, scattered all over the Arcadia (spite of some stiffness and encumberment), justify to me the character which his contemporaries have left us of the writer. I cannot think with the Critic, that Sir Philip Sydney was that *opprobrious thing* which a foolish nobleman in his insolent hostility chose to term him. I call to mind the epitaph made on him, to guide me to juster thoughts of him; and I repose upon the beautiful lines in the 'Friend's Passion for his Astrophel,' printed with the Elegies of Spenser and others.

> You knew—who knew not Astrophel?
> (That I should live to say I knew,
> And have not in possession still!)—
> Things known permit me to renew—
>   Of him you know his merit such,
>   I cannot say—you hear—too much.
>
> Within these woods of Arcady
> He chief delight and pleasure took;
> And on the mountain Partheny,
> Upon the crystal liquid brook,
>   The Muses met him every day,
>   That taught him sing, to write, and say.
>
> When he descended down the mount,
> His personage seemed most divine:
> A thousand graces one might count
> Upon his lovely chearful eyne,
>   To hear him speak, and sweetly smile,
>   You were in Paradise the while.
>
> *A sweet attractive kind of grace;*
> *A full assurance given by looks;*
> *Continual comfort in a face,*
> *The lineaments of Gospel books—*
>   I trow that count'nance cannot lye,
>   Whose thoughts are legible in the eye.
>
>   *   *   *   *   *   *
>
> Above all others this is he,
> Which erst approved in his song,
> That love and honour might agree,
> And that pure love will do no wrong.
>   Sweet saints, it is no sin or blame
>   To love a man of virtuous name.
>
> Did never Love so sweetly breathe
> In any mortal breast before:
> Did never Muse inspire beneath
> A Poet's brain with finer store.
>   He wrote of Love with high conceit,
>   And Beauty rear'd above her height.

Or let any one read the deeper sorrows (grief running into rage) in the Poem,—the last in the collection accompanying the above,—which from internal testimony I believe to be Lord Brooke's,—beginning with 'Silence augmenteth grief,' —and then seriously ask himself, whether the subject of such absorbing and confounding regrets could have been *that thing* which Lord Oxford termed him. *The Last Essays of Elia.* 1823.

CHARACTERS OF DRAMATIC WRITERS CON-TEMPORARY WITH SHAKSPEARE

When I selected for publication, in 1808, Specimens of English Dramatic Poets who lived about the time of Shakspeare, the kind of extracts which I was anxious to give were, not so much passages of wit and humour, though the old plays are rich in such, as scenes of passion, sometimes of the deepest quality, interesting situations, serious descriptions, that which is more nearly allied to poetry than to wit, and to tragic rather than to comic poetry. The plays which I made choice of were, with few exceptions, such as treat of human life and manners, rather than masques and Arcadian pastorals, with their train of abstractions, unimpassioned deities, passionate mortals—Claius, and Medorus, and Amintas, and Amarillis. My leading design was, to illustrate what may be called the moral sense of our ancestors. To shew in what manner they felt, when they placed themselves by the power of imagination in trying circumstances, in the conflicts of duty and passion, or the strife of contending duties; what sort of loves and enmities theirs were; how their griefs were tempered, and their full-swoln joys abated: how much of Shakspeare shines in the great men his contemporaries, and how far in his divine mind and manners he surpassed them and all mankind. I was also desirous to bring together some of the most admired scenes of Fletcher and Massinger, in the estimation of the world the only dramatic poets of that age entitled to be considered after Shakspeare, and, by exhibiting them in the same volume with the more impressive scenes of Old Marlowe, Heywood, Tourneur, Webster, Ford, and others, to shew what we had slighted, while beyond all proportion we had been crying up one or two favourite names. From the desultory criticism which accompanied that publication, I have selected a few which I thought would best stand by themselves, as requiring least immediate reference to the play or passage by which they were suggested.

CHRISTOPHER MARLOWE

Lust's Dominion, or the Lascivious Queen. This tragedy is in King Cambyses' vein; rape, and murder, and superlatives; 'huffing braggart puft lines,' such as the play-writers anterior to Shakspeare are full of, and Pistol but coldly imitates.

Tamburlaine the Great, or the Scythian Shepherd. The lunes of Tamburlaine are perfect midsummer madness. Nebuchadnazar's are mere modest pretensions compared with the thundering vaunts of this Scythian Shepherd. He comes in, drawn by conquered kings, and reproaches these *pampered jades of Asia* that they can *draw but twenty miles a day.* Till I saw this passage with my own eyes, I never believed that it was any thing more than a pleasant burlesque of mine ancient's. But I can assure my readers that it is soberly set down in a play, which their ancestors took to be serious.

Edward the Second. In a very different style from mighty Tamburlaine is the tragedy of Edward the Second. The reluctant pangs of abdicating royalty in Edward furnished hints, which Shakspeare scarcely improved in his Richard the Second; and the death-scene of Marlowe's king moves pity and terror beyond any scene antient or modern with which I am acquainted.

The Rich Jew of Malta. Marlowe's Jew does not approach so near to Shakspeare's, as his Edward the Second does to Richard the Second. Barabas is a mere monster brought in with a large painted nose to please the rabble. He kills in sport, poisons whole nunneries, invents infernal machines. He is just such an exhibition as a century or two earlier might have been played before the Londoners 'by the royal command,' when a general pillage and massacre of the Hebrews had been previously resolved on in the cabinet. It is curious to see a superstition wearing out. The idea of a Jew, which our pious ancestors contemplated with so much horror, has nothing in it now revolting. We have tamed the claws of the beast, and pared its nails, and now we take it to our arms, fondle it, write plays to flatter it; it is visited by princes, affects a taste, patronizes the arts, and is the only liberal and gentlemanlike thing in Christendom.

Doctor Faustus. The growing horrors of Faustus's last scene are awfully marked by the hours and half hours as they expire, and bring him nearer and nearer to the exactment of his dire compact. It is indeed an agony and a fearful colluctation. Marlowe is said to have been tainted with atheistical positions, to have denied God and the Trinity. To such a genius the history of Faustus must have been delectable food: to wander in fields where curiosity is forbidden to go, to approach the dark gulf near enough to look in, to be busied in speculations which are the rottenest part of the core of the fruit that fell from the tree of knowledge[1]. Barabas the Jew, and Faustus the conjurer, are offsprings of a mind which at least delighted to dally with interdicted subjects. They both talk a language which a believer would have been tender of putting into the mouth of a character though but in fiction. But the holiest minds have sometimes not thought it reprehensible to counterfeit impiety in the person of another, to bring Vice upon the stage speaking her own dialect; and, themselves being armed with an unction of self-confident impunity, have not scrupled to handle and touch that familiarly, which would be death to others. Milton in the person of Satan has started speculations hardier than any which the feeble armoury of the atheist ever furnished; and the precise, strait-laced Richardson has strengthened Vice, from the mouth of Lovelace, with entangling sophistries and abstruse pleas against her adversary Virtue, which Sedley, Villiers, and Rochester, wanted depth of libertinism enough to have invented.

Thomas Decker

Old Fortunatus. The humour of a frantic lover, in the scene where Orleans to his friend Galloway defends the passion with which himself, being a prisoner in the English king's court, is enamoured to frenzy of the king's daughter Agripyna, is done to the life. Orleans is as passionate an inamorato as any which Shakspeare ever drew. He is just such another adept in Love's reasons. The sober people of the world are with him

——A swarm of fools
Crowding together to be counted wise.

[1] Error, entering into the world with Sin among us poor Adamites, may be said to spring from the tree of knowledge itself, and from the rotten kernels of that fatal apple.—*Howell's Letters.*

He talks 'pure Biron and Romeo,' he is almost as poetical as they, quite as philosophical, only a little madder. After all, Love's sectaries are a reason unto themselves. We have gone retrograde to the noble heresy, since the days when Sidney proselyted our nation to this mixed health and disease; the kindliest symptom, yet the most alarming crisis in the ticklish state of youth; the nourisher and the destroyer of hopeful wits; the mother of twin births, wisdom and folly, valour and weakness; the servitude above freedom; the gentle mind's religion; the liberal superstition.

The Honest Whore. There is in the second part of this play, where Bellafront, a reclaimed harlot, recounts some of the miseries of her profession, a simple picture of honour and shame, contrasted without violence, and expressed without immodesty, which is worth all the *strong lines* against the harlot's profession, with which both parts of this play are offensively crowded. A satirist is always to be suspected, who, to make vice odious, dwells upon all its acts and minutest circumstances with a sort of relish and retrospective fondness. But so near are the boundaries of panegyric and invective, that a worn-out sinner is sometimes found to make the best declaimer against sin. The same high-seasoned descriptions, which in his unregenerate state served but to inflame his appetites, in his new province of a moralist will serve him, a little turned, to expose the enormity of those appetites in other men. When Cervantes with such proficiency of fondness dwells upon the Don's library, who sees not that he has been a great reader of books of knight-errantry—perhaps was at some time of his life in danger of falling into those very extravagancies which he ridiculed so happily in his hero?

JOHN MARSTON

Antonio and Mellida. The situation of Andrugio and Lucio, in the first part of this tragedy, where Andrugio Duke of Genoa banished his country, with the loss of a son supposed drowned, is cast upon the territory of his mortal enemy the Duke of Venice, with no attendants but Lucio an old nobleman, and a page—resembles that of Lear and Kent in that king's distresses. Andrugio, like Lear, manifests a kinglike impatience, a turbulent greatness, an affected resignation. The enemies which he enters lists to combat, 'Despair and mighty Grief and sharp

Impatience,' and the forces which he brings to vanquish them, 'cornets of horse,' etc. are in the boldest style of allegory. They are such a 'race of mourners' as the 'infection of sorrows loud' in the intellect might beget on some 'pregnant could' in the imagination. The prologue to the second part, for its passionate earnestness, and for the tragic note of preparation which it sounds, might have preceded one of those old tales of Thebes or Pelops' line, which Milton has so highly commended, as free from the common error of the poets in his day, of 'intermixing comic stuff with tragic sadness and gravity, brought in without discretion corruptly to gratify the people.' It is as solemn a preparative as the 'warning voice which he who saw the Apocalyps heard cry.'

What you Will.—O I shall ne'er forget how he went cloath'd. Act I. Scene 1. To judge of the liberality of these notions of dress, we must advert to the days of Gresham, and the consternation which a phenomenon habited like the merchant here described would have excited among the flat round caps and cloth stockings upon 'Change, when those 'original arguments or tokens of a citizen's vocation were in fashion, not more for thrift and usefulness than for distinction and grace.' The blank uniformity to which all professional distinctions in apparel have been long hastening, is one instance of the decay of symbols among us, which, whether it has contributed or not to make us a more intellectual, has certainly made us a less imaginative people. Shakspeare knew the force of signs: a 'malignant and a turban'd Turk.' This 'meal-cap miller,' says the author of God's Revenge against Murder, to express his indignation at an atrocious outrage committed by the miller Pierot upon the person of the fair Marieta.

AUTHOR UNKNOWN

The Merry Devil of Edmonton. The scene in this delightful comedy, in which Jerningham, 'with the true feeling of a zealous friend,' touches the griefs of Mounchensey, seems written to make the reader happy. Few of our dramatists or novelists have attended enough to this. They torture and wound us abundantly. They are economists only in delight. Nothing can be finer, more gentlemanlike, and nobler, than the conversation and compliments of these young men. How delicious is Raymond Mounchensey's forgetting, in his fears, that

2—2

Jerningham has a 'Saint in Essex'; and how sweetly his friend reminds him! I wish it could be ascertained, which there is some grounds for believing, that Michael Drayton was the author of this piece. It would add a worthy appendage to the renown of that Panegyrist of my native Earth; who has gone over her soil, in his Polyolbion, with the fidelity of a herald, and the painful love of a son; who has not left a rivulet, so narrow that it may be stept over, without honourable mention; and has animated hills and streams with life and passion beyond the dreams of old mythology.

THOMAS HEYWOOD

A Woman Killed with Kindness. Heywood is a sort of *prose* Shakspeare. His scenes are to the full as natural and affecting. But we miss *the poet,* that which in Shakspeare always appears out and above the surface of *the nature.* Heywood's characters in this play, for instance, his country gentlemen, etc. are exactly what we see, but of the best kind of what we see, in life. Shakspeare makes us believe, while we are among his lovely creations, that they are nothing but what we are familiar with, as in dreams new things seem old; but we awake, and sigh for the difference.

The English Traveller. Heywood's preface to this play is interesting, as it shews the heroic indifference about the opinion of posterity, which some of these great writers seem to have felt. There is a magnanimity in authorship as in every thing else. His ambition seems to have been confined to the pleasure of hearing the players speak his lines while he lived. It does not appear that he ever contemplated the possibility of being read by after ages. What a slender pittance of fame was motive sufficient to the production of such plays as the English Traveller, the Challenge for Beauty, and the Woman Killed with Kindness! Posterity is bound to take care that a writer loses nothing by such a noble modesty.

THOMAS MIDDLETON AND WILLIAM ROWLEY

A Fair Quarrel. The insipid levelling morality to which the modern stage is tied down, would not admit of such admirable passions as these scenes are filled with. A puritanical obtuseness of sentiment, a stupid infantile goodness, is creeping among us, instead of the vigorous passions, and virtues clad in flesh and blood, with which the old dramatists present us. Those noble and liberal casuists could discern in the differences, the quarrels, the animosities of men, a beauty and truth of moral feeling no less than in the everlastingly inculcated duties of forgiveness and atonement. With us, all is hypocritical meekness. A reconciliation-scene, be the occasion never so absurd, never fails of applause. Our audiences come to the theatre to be complimented on their goodness. They compare notes with the amiable characters in the play, and find a wonderful sympathy of disposition between them. We have a common stock of dramatic morality, out of which a writer may be supplied without the trouble of copying it from originals within his own breast. To know the boundaries of honour, to be judiciously valiant, to have a temperance which shall beget a smoothness in the angry swellings of youth, to esteem life as nothing when the sacred reputation of a parent is to be defended, yet to shake and tremble under a pious cowardice when that ark of an honest confidence is found to be frail and tottering, to feel the true blows of a real disgrace blunting that sword which the imaginary strokes of a supposed false imputation had put so keen an edge upon but lately: to do, or to imagine this done in a feigned story, asks something more of a moral sense, somewhat a greater delicacy of perception in questions of right and wrong, than goes to the writing of two or three hackneyed sentences about the laws of honour as opposed to the laws of the land, or a commonplace against duelling. Yet such things would stand a writer now-a-days in far better stead than Captain Agar and his conscientious honour; and he would be considered as a far better teacher of morality than old Rowley or Middleton, if they were living.

WILLIAM ROWLEY

A New Wonder; a Woman Never Vext. The old play-writers are distinguished by an honest boldness of exhibition, they shew every thing without being ashamed. If a reverse in fortune is to be exhibited, they fairly bring us to the prison-grate and the alms-basket. A poor man on our stage is always a gentleman, he may be known by a peculiar neatness of apparel, and by wearing black. Our delicacy in fact forbids the dramatizing of distress at all. It is never shown in its essential properties; it appears but as the adjunct of some virtue, as something which is to be relieved, from the approbation of which relief the spectators are to derive a certain soothing of self-referred satisfaction. We turn away from the real essences of things to hunt after their relative shadows, moral duties; whereas, if the truth of things were fairly represented, the relative duties might be safely trusted to themselves, and moral philosophy lose the name of a science.

Thomas Middleton

The Witch. Though some resemblance may be traced between the charms in Macbeth, and the incantations in this play, which is supposed to have preceded it, this coincidence will not detract much from the originality of Shakspeare. His witches are distinguished from the witches of Middleton by essential differences. These are creatures to whom man or woman, plotting some dire mischief, might resort for occasional consultation. Those originate deeds of blood, and begin bad impulses to men. From the moment that their eyes first meet with Macbeth's, he is spell-bound. That meeting sways his destiny. He can never break the fascination. These witches can hurt the body, those have power over the soul. Hecate in Middleton has a son, a low buffoon: the hags of Shakspeare have neither child of their own, nor seem to be descended from any parent. They are foul anomalies, of whom we know not whence they are sprung, nor whether they have beginning or ending. As they are without human passions, so they seem to be without human relations. They come with thunder and lightning, and vanish to airy music. This is all we know of them. Except Hecate, they have no *names*; which heightens their mysteriousness. The names, and some of the properties, which the other author has given to his hags, excite smiles. The Weïrd Sisters are serious things. Their presence cannot co-exist with mirth. But, in a lesser degree, the witches of Middleton are fine creations. Their power too is, in some measure, over the mind. They raise jars, jealousies, strifes, 'like a thick scurf' over life.

William Rowley,—Thomas Decker,—John Ford, etc.

The Witch of Edmonton. Mother Sawyer, in this wild play, differs from the hags of both Middleton and Shakspeare. She is the plain traditional old woman witch of our ancestors; poor, deformed, and ignorant; the terror of villages, herself amenable to a justice. That should be a hardy sheriff, with the power of the county at his heels, that would lay hands upon the Weïrd Sisters. They are of another jurisdiction. But upon the common and received opinion, the author (or authors) have engrafted strong fancy. There is something frightfully earnest in her invocations to the Familiar.

CYRIL TOURNEUR

The Revenger's Tragedy. The reality and life of the dialogue, in which Vindici and Hippolito first tempt their mother, and then threaten her with death for consenting to the dishonour of their sister, passes any scenical illusion I ever felt. I never read it but my ears tingle, and I feel a hot blush overspread my cheeks, as if I were presently about to proclaim such malefactions of myself as the brothers here rebuke in their unnatural parent, in words more keen and dagger-like than those which Hamlet speaks to his mother. Such power has the passion of shame truly personated, not only to strike guilty creatures unto the soul, but to 'appal' even those that are 'free.'

JOHN WEBSTER

The Duchess of Malfy. All the several parts of the dreadful apparatus with which the death of the Duchess is ushered in, the waxen images which counterfeit death, the wild masque of madmen, the tomb-maker, the bellman, the living person's dirge, the mortification by degrees,—are not more remote from the conceptions of ordinary vengeance, than the strange character of suffering which they seem to bring upon their victim is out of the imagination of ordinary poets. As they are not like inflictions of this life, so her language seems not of this world. She has lived among horrors till she is become 'native and endowed unto that element.' She speaks the dialect of despair; her tongue has a smatch of Tartarus and the souls in bale. To move a horror skilfully, to touch a soul to the quick, to lay upon fear as much as it can bear, to wean and weary a life till it is ready to drop, and then step in with mortal instruments to take its last forfeit: this only a Webster can do. Inferior geniuses may 'upon horror's head horrors accumulate,' but they cannot do this. They mistake quantity for quality; they 'terrify babes with painted devils'; but they know not how a soul is to be moved. Their terrors want dignity, their affrightments are without decorum.

The White Devil, or Vittoria Corombona. This White Devil of Italy sets off a bad cause so speciously, and pleads with such an innocence-resembling boldness, that we seem to see that matchless beauty of her face which inspires such gay confidence into her, and are ready to expect, when she has done her pleadings, that her very judges, her accusers, the grave ambassadors who sit as spectators, and all the court, will rise and make proffer to defend her in spite of the utmost conviction of her guilt; as the Shepherds in Don Quixote make proffer to follow the beautiful Shepherdess Marcela, 'without making any profit of her manifest resolution made there in their hearing.'

> So sweet and lovely does she make the shame,
> Which, like a canker in the fragrant rose,
> Does spot the beauty of her budding name!

I never saw any thing like the funeral dirge in this play, for the death of Marcello, except the ditty which reminds Ferdinand of his drowned father in the Tempest. As that is of the water, watery; so this is of the earth, earthy. Both have that intenseness of feeling, which seems to resolve itself into the element which it contemplates.

In a note on the Spanish Tragedy in the Specimens [1808] I have said that there is nothing in the undoubted plays of Jonson which would authorize us to suppose that he could have supplied the additions to Hieronymo. I suspected the agency of some more potent spirit. I thought that Webster might have furnished them. They seemed full of that wild, solemn, preternatural cast of grief which bewilders us in the Duchess of Malfy. On second consideration, I think this a hasty criticism. They are more like the overflowing griefs and talking distraction of Titus Andronicus. The sorrows of the Duchess set inward; if she talks, it is little more than soliloquy imitating conversation in a kind of bravery.

JOHN FORD

The Broken Heart. I do not know where to find, in any play, a catastrophe so grand, so solemn, and so surprising, as in this. This is indeed, according to Milton, to describe high passions and high actions. The fortitude of the Spartan boy, who let a beast gnaw out his bowels till he died without expressing a groan, is a faint bodily image of this dilaceration of the spirit, and exenteration of the inmost mind, which Calantha, with a holy violence against her nature, keeps closely covered, till the last duties of a wife and a queen are fulfilled. Stories of martyrdom are but of chains and the stake; a little bodily suffering. These torments

> On the purest spirits prey,
> As on entrails, joints, and limbs,
> With answerable pains, but more intense.

What a noble thing is the soul in its strengths and in its weaknesses! Who would be less weak than Calantha? Who can be so strong? The expression of this transcendant scene almost bears us in imagination to Calvary and the Cross; and we seem to perceive some analogy between the scenical sufferings which we are here contemplating, and the real agonies of that final completion to which we dare no more than hint a reference. Ford was of the first order of poets. He sought for sublimity, not by parcels, in metaphors or visible images, but directly where she has her full residence in the heart of man; in the actions and sufferings of the greatest minds. There is a grandeur of the soul above mountains, seas, and the elements. Even in the poor perverted reason of Giovanni and Annabella, in the play[1] which stands at the head of the modern collection of the works of this author, we discern traces of that fiery particle, which, in the irregular starting from out the road of beaten action, discovers something of a right line even in obliquity, and shews hints of an improveable greatness in the lowest descents and degradations of our nature.

FULKE GREVILLE, LORD BROOKE

Alaham, Mustapha. The two tragedies of Lord Brooke, printed among his poems, might with more propriety have been termed political treatises than plays. Their author has strangely contrived to make passion, character, and interest, of the highest order, subservient to the expression of state dogmas and mysteries. He is nine parts Machiavel and Tacitus, for one part Sophocles or Seneca. In this writer's estimate of the powers of the mind, the understanding must have held a most tyrannical pre-eminence. Whether we look into his plays, or

[1] 'Tis Pity she is a Whore.

his most passionate love-poems, we shall find all frozen and made rigid with intellect. The finest movements of the human heart, the utmost grandeur of which the soul is capable, are essentially comprised in the actions and speeches of Cælica and Camena. Shakspeare, who seems to have had a peculiar delight in contemplating womanly perfection, whom for his many sweet images of female excellence all women are in an especial manner bound to love, has not raised the ideal of the female character higher than Lord Brooke, in these two women, has done. But it requires a study equivalent to the learning of a new language to understand their meaning when they speak. It is indeed hard to hit:

> Much like thy riddle, Samson, in one day
> Or seven though one should musing sit.

It is as if a being of pure intellect should take upon him to express the emotions of our sensitive natures. There would be all knowledge, but sympathetic expressions would be wanting.

BEN JONSON

The Case is Altered. The passion for wealth has worn out much of its grossness in tract of time. Our ancestors certainly conceived of money as able to confer a distinct gratification in itself, not considered simply as a symbol of wealth. The old poets, when they introduce a miser, make him address his gold as his mistress; as something to be seen, felt, and hugged; as capable of satisfying two of the senses at least. The substitution of a thin, unsatisfying medium in the place of the good old tangible metal, has made avarice quite a Platonic affection in comparison with the seeing, touching, and handling-pleasures of the old Chrysophilites. A bank-note can no more satisfy the touch of a true sensualist in this passion, than Creusa could return her husband's embrace in the shades. See the Cave of Mammon in Spenser; Barabas's contemplation of his wealth in the Rich Jew of Malta; Luke's raptures in the City Madam; the idolatry and absolute gold-worship of the miser Jaques in this early comic production of Ben Jonson's. Above all hear Guzman, in that excellent old translation of the Spanish Rogue, expatiate on the 'ruddy cheeks of your golden ruddocks, your Spanish pistolets, your plump and full-faced Portuguese, and your clear-skinned pieces of eight of Castile,' which he and his fellows the beggars kept secret to themselves, and did 'privately enjoy in a plentiful manner.' 'For to have them, to pay them away, is not to enjoy them; to enjoy them, is to have them lying by us; having no other need of them than to use them for the clearing of the eye-sight, and the comforting of our senses. These we did carry about with us, sewing them in some patches of our doublets near unto the heart, and as close to the skin as we could handsomely quilt them in, holding them to be restorative.'

Poetaster. This Roman play seems written to confute those enemies of Ben in his own days and ours, who have said that he made a pedantical use of his learning. He has here revived the whole Court of Augustus, by a learned spell. We are admitted to the society of the illustrious dead. Virgil, Horace, Ovid, Tibullus, converse in our own tongue more finely and poetically than they were used to express themselves in their native Latin. Nothing can be imagined more elegant, refined, and court-like, than the scenes between this Louis the Four-teenth of antiquity and his literati. The whole essence and secret of that kind of intercourse is contained therein. The economical liberality by which greatness, seeming to waive some part of its prerogative, takes care to lose none of the essentials; the prudential liberties of an inferior, which flatter by commanded boldness and soothe with complimentary sin-cerity. These, and a thousand beautiful passages from his New Inn, his Cynthia's Revels, and from those numerous court-masques and entertainments which he was in the daily habit of furnishing, might be adduced to shew the poetical fancy and elegance of mind of the supposed rugged old bard.

Alchemist. The judgment is perfectly overwhelmed by the torrent of images, words, and book-knowledge, with which Epicure Mammon (Act 2, Scene 2) confounds and stuns his incredulous hearer. They come pouring out like the successive falls of Nilus. They 'doubly redouble strokes upon the foe.' Description outstrides proof. We are made to believe effects before we have testimony for their causes. If there is no one image which attains the height of the sublime, yet the con-fluence and assemblage of them all produces a result equal to the grandest poetry. The huge Zerxean army countervails against single Achilles. Epicure Mammon is the most deter-mined offspring of its author. It has the whole 'matter and copy of the father—eye, nose, lip, the trick of his frown.' It

is just such a swaggerer as contemporaries have described old
Ben to be. Meercraft, Bobadil, the Host of the New Inn, have
all his image and superscription. But Mammon is arrogant
pretension personified. Sir Samson Legend, in Love for Love,
is such another lying, overbearing character, but he does not
come up to Epicure Mammon. What a 'towering bravery'
there is in his sensuality! he affects no pleasure under a Sultan.
It is as if 'Egypt with Assyria strove in luxury.'

GEORGE CHAPMAN

*Bussy D'Ambois, Byron's Conspiracy, Byron's Tragedy, etc.,
etc.* Webster has happily characterised the 'full and heightened
style' of Chapman, who, of all the English play-writers, perhaps
approaches nearest to Shakspeare in the descriptive and
didactic, in passages which are less purely dramatic. He could
not go out of himself, as Shakspeare could shift at pleasure, to
inform and animate other existences, but in himself he had an
eye to perceive and a soul to embrace all forms and modes of
being. He would have made a great epic poet, if indeed he has
not abundantly shewn himself to be one; for his Homer is not
so properly a translation as the stories of Achilles and Ulysses
re-written. The earnestness and passion which he has put into
every part of these poems, would be incredible to a reader of
mere modern translations. His almost Greek zeal for the glory
of his heroes can only be paralleled by that fierce spirit of
Hebrew bigotry, with which Milton, as if personating one of
the zealots of the old law, clothed himself when he sat down
to paint the acts of Samson against the uncircumcised. The
great obstacle to Chapman's translations being read, is their
unconquerable quaintness. He pours out in the same breath
the most just and natural, and the most violent and crude
expressions. He seems to grasp at whatever words come first
to hand while the enthusiasm is upon him, as if all other must
be inadequate to the divine meaning. But passion (the all in
all in poetry) is every where present, raising the low, dignifying
the mean, and putting sense into the absurd. He makes his
readers glow, weep, tremble, take any affection which he
pleases, be moved by words, or in spite of them, be disgusted
and overcome their disgust.

FRANCIS BEAUMONT.—JOHN FLETCHER

Maid's Tragedy. One characteristic of the excellent old poets is, their being able to bestow grace upon subjects which naturally do not seem susceptible of any. I will mention two instances. Zelmane in the Arcadia of Sidney, and Helena in the All's Well that Ends Well of Shakspeare. What can be more unpromising at first sight, than the idea of a young man disguising himself in women's attire, and passing himself off for a woman among women; and that for a long space of time? Yet Sir Philip has preserved so matchless a decorum, that neither does Pryocles' manhood suffer any stain for the effeminacy of Zelmane, nor is the respect due to the princesses at all diminished when the deception comes to be known. In the sweetly constituted mind of Sir Philip Sidney, it seems as if no ugly thought or unhandsome meditation could find a harbour. He turned all that he touched into images of honour and virtue. Helena in Shakspeare is a young woman seeking a man in marriage. The ordinary rules of courtship are reversed, the habitual feelings are crossed. Yet with such exquisite address this dangerous subject is handled, that Helena's forwardness loses her no honour; delicacy dispenses with its laws in her favour, and nature, in her single case, seems content to suffer a sweet violation. Aspatia, in the Maid's Tragedy, is a character equally difficult, with Helena, of being managed with grace. She too is a slighted woman, refused by the man who had once engaged to marry her. Yet it is artfully contrived, that while we pity we respect her, and she descends without degradation. Such wonders true poetry and passion can do, to confer dignity upon subjects which do not seem capable of it. But Aspatia must not be compared at all points with Helena; she does not so absolutely predominate over her situation but she suffers some diminution, some abatement of the full lustre of the female character, which Helena never does. Her character has many degrees of sweetness, some of delicacy; but it has weakness, which, if we do not despise, we are sorry for. After all, Beaumont and Fletcher were but an inferior sort of Shakspeares and Sidneys.

Philaster. The character of Bellario must have been extremely popular in its day. For many years after the date of Philaster's first exhibition on the stage, scarce a play can be found without one of these women pages in it, following in the train of some pre-engaged lover, calling on the gods to bless her happy rival (his mistress), whom no doubt she secretly curses in her heart, giving rise to many pretty *equivoques* by the way on the confusion of sex, and either made happy at last by some surprising turn of fate, or dismissed with the joint pity of the lovers and the audience. Donne has a copy of verses to his mistress, dissuading her from a resolution which she seems to have taken up from some of these scenical representations, of following him abroad as a page. It is so earnest, so weighty, so rich in poetry, in sense, in wit, and pathos, that it deserves to be read as a solemn close in future to all such sickly fancies as he there deprecates.

JOHN FLETCHER

Thierry and Theodoret. The scene where Ordella offers her life a sacrifice, that the king of France may not be childless, I have always considered as the finest in all Fletcher, and Ordella to be the most perfect notion of the female heroic character, next to Calantha in the Broken Heart. She is a piece of sainted nature. Yet noble as the whole passage is, it must be confessed that the manner of it, compared with Shakspeare's finest scenes, is faint and languid. Its motion is circular, not progressive. Each line revolves on itself in a sort of separate orbit. They do not join into one another like a running-hand. Fletcher's ideas moved slow; his versification, though sweet, is tedious, it stops at every turn; he lays line upon line, making up one after the other, adding image to image so deliberately, that we see their junctures. Shakspeare mingles everything, runs line into line, embarrasses sentences and metaphors; before one idea has burst its shell, another is hatched and clamorous for disclosure. Another striking difference between Fletcher and Shakspeare, is the fondness of the former for unnatural and violent situations. He seems to have thought that nothing great could be produced in an ordinary way. The chief incidents in some of his most admired tragedies shew this[1]. Shakspeare had nothing of this contortion in his mind, none of that craving after violent situations, and flights of strained and improbable virtue, which I think always betrays an imperfect moral sensibility. The wit of Fletcher is excellent[2] like his serious scenes,

---

[1] Wife for a Month, Cupid's Revenge, Double Marriage, etc.
[2] Wit without Money, and his comedies generally.

but there is something strained and far-fetched in both. He is too mistrustful of Nature, he always goes a little on one side of her. Shakspeare chose her without a reserve: and had riches, power, understanding, and length of days, with her, for a dowry.

Faithful Shepherdess. If all the parts of this delightful pastoral had been in unison with its many innocent scenes and sweet lyric intermixtures, it had been a poem fit to vie with Comus or the Arcadia, to have been put into the hands of boys and virgins, to have made matter for young dreams, like the loves of Hermia and Lysander. But a spot is on the face of this Diana. Nothing short of infatuation could have driven Fletcher upon mixing with this 'blessedness' such an ugly deformity as Cloe, the wanton shepherdess! If Cloe was meant to set off Clorin by contrast, Fletcher should have known that such weeds by juxta-position do not set off, but kill sweet flowers.

PHILIP MASSINGER.—THOMAS DECKER

The Virgin Martyr. This play has some beauties of so very high an order, that with all my respect for Massinger, I do not think he had poetical enthusiasm capable of rising up to them. His associate Decker, who wrote Old Fortunatus, had poetry enough for any thing. The very impurities which obtrude themselves among the sweet pieties of this play, like Satan among the Sons of Heaven, have a strength of contrast, a raciness, and a glow, in them, which are beyond Massinger. They are to the religion of the rest what Caliban is to Miranda.

PHILIP MASSINGER.—THOMAS MIDDLETON.— WILLIAM ROWLEY

Old Law. There is an exquisiteness of moral sensibility, making one's eyes to gush out tears of delight, and a poetical strangeness in the circumstances of this sweet tragi-comedy, which are unlike anything in the dramas which Massinger wrote alone. The pathos is of a subtler edge. Middleton and Rowley, who assisted in it, had both of them finer geniuses than their associate.

James Shirley

Claims a place amongst the worthies of this period, not so much
for any transcendant talent in himself, as that he was the last
of a great race, all of whom spoke nearly the same language,
and had a set of moral feelings and notions in common. A
new language, and quite a new turn of tragic and comic
interest, came in with the Restoration.

From the *Works* of 1818.

THE ELIZABETHAN DRAMATISTS

These old play-wrights invested their bad characters with
notions of good, which could by no possibility have co-existed
with their actions. Without a soul of goodness in himself, how
could Shakspere's *Richard the Third* have lit upon those sweet
phrases and inducements by which he attempts to win over
the dowager queen to let him wed her daughter. It is not
nature's nature, but imagination's substituted nature, which
does almost as well in a fiction.

Not a third part of the treasures of old English dramatic
literature has been exhausted. Are we afraid that the genius
of Shakspeare would suffer in our estimate by the disclosure?
He would indeed be somewhat lessened as a miracle and a
prodigy. But he would lose no height by the confession. When
a giant is shown to us, does it detract from the curiosity to be
told that he has at home a gigantic brood of brethren, less
only than himself? Along *with* him, not *from* him, sprang up
the race of mighty dramatists, who, compared with the Otways
and Rowes that followed, were as Miltons to a Young or an
Akenside. That he was their elder brother, not their parent, is
evident from the fact of the very few direct imitations of him
to be found in their writings. Webster, Dekker, Heywood, and
the rest of his great contemporaries went on their own ways,
and followed their individual impulses, not blindly prescribing
to themselves his tract. Marlowe, the true (though imperfect)
father of our *tragedy*, preceded him. The *comedy* of Fletcher is
essentially unlike to that of his. 'Tis out of no detracting
spirit that I speak thus, for the plays of Shakspeare have been

the strongest and the sweetest food of my mind from infancy;
but I resent the comparative obscurity in which some of his
most valuable co-operators remain, who were his dear intimates,
his stage and his chamber-fellows while he lived, and to whom
his gentle spirit doubtlessly then awarded the full portion of
their genius, as from them towards himself appears to have
been no grudging of his acknowledged excellence.

Notes, etc., to Extracts from the Garrick Plays. 1827.

CHAPMAN

I have just finished Chapman's Homer. Did you ever read
it? it has the continuous power of interesting you all along,
like a rapid original, more than any; and in the uncommon
excellence of the more finished parts goes beyond Fairfax or
any of 'em. The metre is fourteen syllables, and capable of all
sweetness and grandeur. Cowper's blank verse detains you
every step with some heavy Miltonism; Chapman gallops off
with you his own free pace. Take a simile for example. The
council breaks up—

> Being abroad, the earth was overlaid
> With flockers to them, that came forth; as when of frequent bees
> Swarms rise out of a hollow rock, repairing the degrees
> *Of their egression endlessly, with ever rising new*
> From forth their sweet nest; as their store, still as it faded, grew,
> *And never would cease sending forth clusters to the spring,*
> They still crowd out so; this flock here, that there, belabouring
> The loaded flowers. So, etc., etc.

What *endless egression of phrases* the dog commands!

Letter to Coleridge, Oct. 23, 1802.

Can any one read the pert, modern, Frenchfied notes, etc.,
in Pope's translation, and contrast them with solemn weighty
prefaces of Chapman, writing in full faith, as he evidently does,
of the plenary inspiration of his author—worshipping his
meanest scraps and relics as divine—without one sceptical
misgiving of their authenticity, and doubt which was the
properest to expound Homer to his' countrymen. Reverend
Chapman! you have read his hymn to Pan (the Homeric)—
why, it is Milton's blank verse clothed with rhyme! *Paradise
Lost* could scarce lose, could it be so accoutred.
I shall die in the belief that he has improved upon Homer,

in the *Odyssey* in particular—the disclosure of Ulysses of himself to Alcinous—his previous behaviour at the song of the stern strife arising between Achilles and himself (how it raised him above the *Iliad* Ulysses!)—but you know all these things quite as well as I do. But what a deaf ear old C. would have turned to the doubters in Homer's real personality! He apparently believed all the fables of Homer's birth, etc., etc.

Letter to C. A. Elton, Aug. 1824 (?).

Bussy D'Ambois: A Tragedy, 1607. [D'Ambois invokes a Spirit of Intelligence, to reveal to him the fate of Tamyra, whose intrigue with him has been discovered by her Husband.]

This calling upon Light and Darkness for information, but, above all, the description of the Spirit—'Threw his changed countenance headlong into clouds'—is tremendous, to the curdling of the blood. I know nothing in Poetry like it.

Notes, etc., to Extracts from the Garrick Plays. 1827.

ON THE TRAGEDIES OF SHAKSPEARE, CONSIDERED
WITH REFERENCE TO THEIR FITNESS FOR STAGE
REPRESENTATION. 1811

Taking a turn the other day in the Abbey, I was struck with the affected attitude of a figure, which I do not remember to have seen before, and which upon examination proved to be a whole-length of the celebrated Mr Garrick. Though I would not go so far with some good catholics abroad as to shut players altogether out of consecrated ground, yet I own I was not a little scandalized at the introduction of theatrical airs and gestures into a place set apart to remind us of the saddest realities. Going nearer, I found inscribed under this harlequin figure the following lines:

> To paint fair Nature, by divine command,
> Her magic pencil in his glowing hand,
> A Shakspeare rose: then, to expand his fame
> Wide o'er this breathing world, a Garrick came.
> Though sunk in death the forms the Poet drew,
> The Actor's genius bade them breathe anew;
> Though, like the bard himself, in night they lay,
> Immortal Garrick call'd them back to day:
> And till Eternity with power sublime
> Shall mark the mortal hour of hoary Time,
> Shakspeare and Garrick like twin-stars shall shine,
> And earth irradiate with a beam divine.

It would be an insult to my readers' understandings to attempt any thing like a criticism on this farrago of false thoughts and nonsense. But the reflection it led me into was a kind of wonder, how, from the days of the actor here celebrated to our own, it should have been the fashion to compliment every performer in his turn, that has had the luck to please the town in any of the great characters of Shakspeare, with the notion of possessing a *mind congenial with the poet's*: how people should come thus unaccountably to confound the power of originating poetical images and conceptions with the faculty of being able to read or recite the same when put into words[1]; or what connection that absolute mastery over the heart and soul of man, which a great dramatic poet possesses, has with those low tricks upon the eye and ear, which a player by observing a few general effects, which some common passion, as grief, anger, etc. usually has upon the gestures and exterior, can so easily compass. To know the internal workings and movements of a great mind, of an Othello or a Hamlet for instance, the *when* and the *why* and the *how far* they should be moved; to what pitch a passion is becoming; to give the reins and to pull in the curb exactly at the moment when the drawing in or the slackening is most graceful; seems to demand a reach of intellect of a vastly different extent from that which is employed upon the bare imitation of the signs of these passions in the countenance or gesture, which signs are usually observed to be most lively and emphatic in the weaker sort of minds, and which signs can after all but indicate some passion, as I said before, anger, or grief, generally; but of the motives and grounds of the passion, wherein it differs from the same passion in low and vulgar natures, of these the actor can give no more idea by his face or gesture than the eye (without a metaphor) can speak, or the muscles utter intelligible sounds. But such is the instantaneous nature of the impressions which we take in at the eye and ear at a playhouse, compared with the slow apprehension oftentimes of the understanding in

[1] It is observable that we fall into this confusion only in *dramatic* recitations. We never dream that the gentleman who reads Lucretius in public with great applause, is therefore a great poet and philosopher; nor do we find that Tom Davies, the bookseller, who is recorded to have recited the Paradise Lost better than any man in England in his day (though I cannot help thinking there must be some mistake in this tradition), was therefore, by his intimate friends, set upon a level with Milton.

reading, that we are apt not only to sink the play-writer in
the consideration which we pay to the actor, but even to
identify in our minds in a perverse manner, the actor with
the character which he represents. It is difficult for a frequent
playgoer to disembarrass the idea of Hamlet from the person
and voice of Mr K. We speak of Lady Macbeth, while we
are in reality thinking of Mrs S. Nor is this confusion inci-
dental alone to unlettered persons, who, not possessing the
advantage of reading, are necessarily dependent upon the stage-
player for all the pleasure which they can receive from the
drama, and to whom the very idea of *what an author is* cannot be
made comprehensible without some pain and perplexity of mind:
the error is one from which persons otherwise not meanly
lettered, find it almost impossible to extricate themselves.

Never let me be so ungrateful as to forget the very high
degree of satisfaction which I received some years back from
seeing for the first time a tragedy of Shakspeare performed, in
which these two great performers sustained the principal parts.
It seemed to embody and realize conceptions which had hitherto
assumed no distinct shape. But dearly do we pay all our life
after for this juvenile pleasure, this sense of distinctness.
When the novelty is past, we find to our cost that instead of
realizing an idea, we have only materialized and brought down
a fine vision to the standard of flesh and blood. We have let
go a dream, in quest of an unattainable substance.

How cruelly this operates upon the mind, to have its free
conceptions thus crampt and pressed down to the measure of
a strait-lacing actuality, may be judged from that delightful
sensation of freshness, with which we turn to those plays of
Shakspeare which have escaped being performed, and to those
passages in the acting plays of the same writer which have
happily been left out in performance. How far the very custom
of hearing any thing *spouted*, withers and blows upon a fine
passage, may be seen in those speeches from Henry the Fifth,
etc. which are current in the mouths of school-boys from their
being to be found in *Enfield Speakers*, and such kind of books.
I confess myself utterly unable to appreciate that celebrated
soliloquy in Hamlet, beginning 'To be or not to be,' or to tell
whether it be good, bad, or indifferent, it has been so handled
and pawed about by declamatory boys and men, and torn so
inhumanly from its living place and principle of continuity in
the play, till it is become to me a perfect dead member.

It may seem a paradox, but I cannot help being of opinion
that the plays of Shakspeare are less calculated for performance on a stage, than those of almost any other dramatist
whatever. Their distinguished excellence is a reason that they
should be so. There is so much in them, which comes not
under the province of acting, with which eye, and tone, and
gesture, have nothing to do.

The glory of the scenic art is to personate passion, and the
turns of passion; and the more coarse and palpable the passion
is, the more hold upon the eyes and ears of the spectators
the performer obviously possesses. For this reason, scolding
scenes, scenes where two persons talk themselves into a fit of
fury, and then in a surprising manner talk themselves out of
it again, have always been the most popular upon our stage.
And the reason is plain, because the spectators are here most
palpably appealed to, they are the proper judges in this war of
words, they are the legitimate ring that should be formed
round such 'intellectual prize-fighters.' Talking is the direct
object of the imitation here. But in all the best dramas, and in
Shakspeare above all, how obvious it is, that the form of
speaking, whether it be in soliloquy or dialogue, is only a
medium, and often a highly artificial one, for putting the
reader or spectator into possession of that knowledge of the
inner structure and workings of mind in a character, which
he could otherwise never have arrived at *in that form of composition* by any gift short of intuition. We do here as we do
with novels written in the *epistolary form*. How many impro-
prieties, perfect solecisms in letter-writing, do we put up with
in Clarissa and other books, for the sake of the delight which
that form upon the whole gives us.

But the practice of stage representation reduces every thing
to a controversy of elocution. Every character, from the
boisterous blasphemings of Bajazet to the shrinking timidity
of womanhood, must play the orator. The love-dialogues of
Romeo and Juliet, those silver-sweet sounds of lovers' tongues
by night; the more intimate and sacred sweetness of nuptial
colloquy between an Othello or a Posthumus with their married
wives, all those delicacies which are so delightful in the reading,
as when we read of those youthful dalliances in Paradise—

As beseem'd
Fair couple link'd in happy nuptial league
Alone:

by the inherent fault of stage representation, how are these things sullied and turned from their very nature by being exposed to a large assembly; when such speeches as Imogen addresses to her lord, come drawling out of the mouth of a hired actress, whose courtship, though nominally addressed to the personated Posthumus, is manifestly aimed at the spectators, who are to judge of her endearments and her returns of love.

The character of Hamlet is perhaps that by which, since the days of Betterton, a succession of popular performers have had the greatest ambition to distinguish themselves. The length of the part may be one of their reasons. But for the character itself, we find it in a play, and therefore we judge it a fit subject of dramatic representation. The play itself abounds in maxims and reflexions beyond any other, and therefore we consider it as a proper vehicle for conveying moral instruction. But Hamlet himself—what does he suffer meanwhile by being dragged forth as a public schoolmaster, to give lectures to the crowd! Why, nine parts in ten of what Hamlet does, are transactions between himself and his moral sense, they are the effusions of his solitary musings, which he retires to holes and corners and the most sequestered parts of the palace to pour forth; or rather, they are the silent meditations with which his bosom is bursting, reduced to *words* for the sake of the reader, who must else remain ignorant of what is passing there. These profound sorrows, these light-and-noise-abhorring ruminations, which the tongue scarce dares utter to deaf walls and chambers, how can they be represented by a gesticulating actor, who comes and mouths them out before an audience, making four hundred people his confidants at once? I say not that it is the fault of the actor so to do; he must pronounce them *ore rotundo*, he must accompany them with his eye, he must insinuate them into his auditory by some trick of eye, tone, or gesture, or he fails. *He must be thinking all the while of his appearance, because he knows that all the while the spectators are judging of it*. And this is the way to represent the shy, negligent, retiring Hamlet.

It is true that there is no other mode of conveying a vast quantity of thought and feeling to a great portion of the audience, who otherwise would never earn it for themselves by reading, and the intellectual acquisition gained this way may, for aught I know, be inestimable; but I am not arguing that Hamlet should not be acted, but how much Hamlet is

made another thing by being acted. I have heard much of the
wonders which Garrick performed in this part; but as I never
saw him, I must have leave to doubt whether the representation
of such a character came within the province of his art. Those
who tell me of him, speak of his eye, of the magic of his eye, and
of his commanding voice: physical properties, vastly desirable
in an actor, and without which he can never insinuate meaning
into an auditory,—but what have they to do with Hamlet?
what have they to do with intellect? In fact, the things aimed
at in theatrical representation, are to arrest the spectator's eye
upon the form and the gesture, and so to gain a more favour-
able hearing to what is spoken: it is not what the character is,
but how he looks; not what he says, but how he speaks it. I
see no reason to think that if the play of Hamlet were written
over again by some such writer as Banks or Lillo, retaining
the process of the story, but totally omitting all the poetry of
it, all the divine features of Shakspeare, his stupendous intellect; and only taking care to give us enough of passionate
dialogue, which Banks or Lillo were never at a loss to furnish;
I see not how the effect could be much different upon an
audience, nor how the actor has it in his power to represent
Shakspeare to us differently from his representation of Banks
or Lillo. Hamlet would still be a youthful accomplished
prince, and must be gracefully personated; he might be puzzled
in his mind, wavering in his conduct, seemingly-cruel to
Ophelia, he might see a ghost, and start at it, and address it
kindly when he found it to be his father; all this in the poorest
and most homely language of the servilest creeper after nature
that ever consulted the palate of an audience; without troubling
Shakspeare for the matter: and I see not but there would be
room for all the power which an actor has, to display itself.
All the passions and changes of passion might remain: for
those are much less difficult to write or act than is thought, it
is a trick easy to be attained, it is but rising or falling a note or
two in the voice, a whisper with a significant foreboding look
to announce its approach, and so contagious the counterfeit
appearance of any emotion is, that let the words be what they
will, the look and tone shall carry it off and make it pass for
deep skill in the passions.

It is common for people to talk of Shakspeare's plays being
so natural; that every body can understand him. They are
natural indeed, they are grounded deep in nature, so deep that

the depth of them lies out of the reach of most of us. You shall hear the same persons say that George Barnwell is very natural, and Othello is very natural, that they are both very deep; and to them they are the same kind of thing. At the one they sit and shed tears, because a good sort of young man is tempted by a naughty woman to commit *a trifling peccadillo*, the murder of an uncle or so[1], that is all, and so comes to an untimely end, which is *so moving*; and at the other, because a blackamoor in a fit of jealousy kills his innocent white wife: and the odds are that ninety-nine out of a hundred would willingly behold the same catastrophe happen to both the heroes, and have thought the rope more due to Othello than to Barnwell. For of the texture of Othello's mind, the inward construction marvellously laid open with all its strengths and weaknesses, its heroic confidences and its human misgivings, its agonies of hate springing from the depths of love, they see no more than the spectators at a cheaper rate, who pay their pennies a-piece to look through the man's telescope in Leicester-fields, see into the inward plot and topography of the moon. Some dim thing or other they see, they see an actor personating a passion, of grief, or anger, for instance, and they recognize it as a copy of the usual external effects of such passions; for at least as being true to *that symbol of the emotion which passes current at the theatre for it*, for it is often no more than that: but of the grounds of the passion, its correspondence to a great or heroic nature, which is the only worthy object of tragedy,—that common auditors know any thing of this, or can have any such notions dinned into them by the mere strength of an actor's lungs,—that apprehensions foreign to them should be thus

[1] If this note could hope to meet the eye of any of the Managers, I would intreat and beg of them, in the name of both the Galleries, that this insult upon the morality of the common people of London should cease to be eternally repeated in the holiday weeks. Why are the 'Prentices of this famous and well-governed city, instead of an amusement, to be treated over and over again with the nauseous sermon of George Barnwell? Why *at the end of their vistoes* are we to place the *gallows*? Were I an uncle, I should not much like a nephew of mine to have such an example placed before his eyes. It is really making uncle-murder too trivial to exhibit it as done upon such slight motives;—it is attributing too much to such characters as Millwood;—it is putting things into the heads of good young men, which they would never otherwise have dreamed of. Uncles that think any thing of their lives, should fairly petition the Chamberlain against it.

infused into them by storm, I can neither believe, nor understand how it can be possible.

We talk of Shakspeare's admirable observation of life, when we should feel, that not from a petty inquisition into those cheap and every-day characters which surrounded him, as they surround us, but from his own mind, which was, to borrow a phrase of Ben Jonson's, the very 'sphere of humanity,' he fetched those images of virtue and of knowledge, of which every one of us recognizing a part, think we comprehend in our natures the whole; and oftentimes mistake the powers which he positively creates in us, for nothing more than indigenous faculties of our own minds which only waited the application of corresponding virtues in him to return a full and clear echo of the same.

To return to Hamlet.—Among the distinguishing features of that wonderful character, one of the most interesting (yet painful) is that soreness of mind which makes him treat the intrusions of Polonius with harshness, and that asperity which he puts on in his interviews with Ophelia. These tokens of an unhinged mind (if they be not mixed in the latter case with a profound artifice of love, to alienate Ophelia by affected discourtesies, so to prepare her mind for the breaking off of that loving intercourse, which can no longer find a place amidst business so serious as that which he has to do) are parts of his character, which to reconcile with our admiration of Hamlet, the most patient consideration of his situation is no more than necessary; they are what we *forgive afterwards*, and explain by the whole of his character, but *at the time* they are harsh and unpleasant. Yet such is the actor's necessity of giving strong blows to the audience, that I have never seen a player in this character, who did not exaggerate and strain to the utmost these ambiguous features,—these temporary deformities in the character. They make him express a vulgar scorn at Polonius which utterly degrades his gentility, and which no explanation can render palateable; they make him shew contempt, and curl up the nose at Ophelia's father,—contempt in its very grossest and most hateful form; but they get applause by it: it is natural, people say; that is, the words are scornful, and the actor expresses scorn, and that they can judge of: but why so much scorn, and of that sort, they never think of asking.

So to Ophelia.—All the Hamlets that I have ever seen, rant and rave at her as if she had committed some great crime, and the audience are highly pleased, because the words of the part are satirical, and they are enforced by the strongest expression of satirical indignation of which the face and voice are capable. But then, whether Hamlet is likely to have put on such brutal appearances to a lady whom he loved so dearly, is never thought on. The truth is, that in all such deep affections as had subsisted between Hamlet and Ophelia, there is a stock of *supererogatory love*, (if I may venture to use the expression) which in any great grief of heart, especially where that which preys upon the mind cannot be communicated, confers a kind of indulgence upon the grieved party to express itself, even to its heart's dearest object, in the language of a temporary aliena-tion; but it is not alienation, it is a distraction purely, and so it always makes itself to be felt by that object: it is not anger, but grief assuming the appearance of anger,—love awkwardly counterfeiting hate, as sweet countenances when they try to frown: but such sternness and fierce disgust as Hamlet is made to shew, is no counterfeit, but the real face of absolute aversion, —of irreconcileable alienation. It may be said he puts on the madman; but then he should only so far put on this counterfeit lunacy as his own real distraction will give him leave; that is, incompletely, imperfectly; not in that confirmed practised way, like a master of his art, or, as Dame Quickly would say, 'like one of those harlotry players.'

I mean no disrespect to any actor, but the sort of pleasure which Shakspeare's plays give in the acting seems to me not at all to differ from that which the audience receive from those of other writers; and, *they being in themselves essentially so different from all others*, I must conclude that there is something in the nature of acting which levels all distinctions. And in fact, who does not speak indifferently of the Gamester and of Macbeth as fine stage performances, and praise the Mrs Beverley in the same way as the Lady Macbeth of Mrs S.? Belvidera, and Calista, and Isabella, and Euphrasia, are they less liked than Imogen, or than Juliet, or than Desdemona? Are they not spoken of and remembered in the same way? Is not the female performer as great (as they call it) in one as in the other? Did not Garrick shine, and was not he ambitious of shining in every drawling tragedy that his wretched day produced,—the productions of the Hills and the Murphys and the Browns,—and shall he have that honour to dwell in our minds for ever as an inseparable concomitant with Shakspeare?

A kindred mind! O who can read that affecting sonnet of
Shakspeare which alludes to his profession as a player:—

> Oh for my sake do you with Fortune chide,
> The guilty goddess of my harmful deeds,
> That did not better for my life provide
> Than public means which public custom breeds—
> Thence comes it that my name receives a brand;
> And almost thence my nature is subdued
> To what it works in, like the dyer's hand—

Or that other confession:—

> Alas! 'tis true, I have gone here and there,
> And made myself a motly to thy view,
> Gor'd mine own thoughts, sold cheap what is most dear—

Who can read these instances of jealous self-watchfulness in
our sweet Shakspeare, and dream of any congeniality between
him and one that, by every tradition of him, appears to have
been as mere a player as ever existed; to have had his mind
tainted with the lowest players' vices,—envy and jealousy, and
miserable cravings after applause; one who in the exercise of
his profession was jealous even of the women-performers that
stood in his way; a manager full of managerial tricks and
stratagems and finesse: that any resemblance should be
dreamed of between him and Shakspeare,—Shakspeare who,
in the plenitude and consciousness of his own powers, could
with that noble modesty, which we can neither imitate nor
appreciate, express himself thus of his own sense of his own
defects:—

> Wishing me like to one more rich in hope,
> Featur'd like him, like him with friends possest;
> Desiring *this man's art, and that man's scope.*

I am almost disposed to deny to Garrick the merit of being
an admirer of Shakspeare. A true lover of his excellencies he
certainly was not; for would any true lover of them have
admitted into his matchless scenes such ribald trash as Tate
and Cibber, and the rest of them, that

> With their darkness durst affront his light,

have foisted into the acting plays of Shakspeare? I believe it
impossible that he could have had a proper reverence for
Shakspeare, and have condescended to go through that inter-
polated scene in Richard the Third, in which Richard tries to
break his wife's heart by telling her he loves another woman,
and says, 'if she survives this she is immortal.' Yet I doubt

not he delivered this vulgar stuff with as much anxiety of emphasis as any of the genuine parts; and for acting, it is as well calculated as any. But we have seen the part of Richard lately produce great fame to an actor by his manner of playing it, and it lets us into the secret of acting, and of popular judgments of Shakspeare derived from acting. Not one of the spectators who have witnessed Mr C.'s exertions in that part, but has come away with a proper conviction that Richard is a very wicked man, and kills little children in their beds, with something like the pleasure which the giants and ogres in children's books are represented to have taken in that practice; moreover, that he is very close and shrewd and devilish cunning, for you could see that by his eye.

But is in fact this the impression we have in reading the Richard of Shakspeare? Do we feel any thing like disgust, as we do at that butcher-like representation of him that passes for him on the stage? A horror at his crimes blends with the effect which we feel, but how is it qualified, how is it carried off, by the rich intellect which he displays, his resources, his wit, his buoyant spirits, his vast knowledge and insight into characters, the poetry of his part,—not an atom of all which is made perceivable in Mr C.'s way of acting it. Nothing but his crimes, his actions, is visible; they are prominent and staring; the murderer stands out, but where is the lofty genius, the man of vast capacity,—the profound, the witty, accomplished Richard?

The truth is, the Characters of Shakspeare are so much the objects of meditation rather than of interest or curiosity as to their actions, that while we are reading any of his great criminal characters,—Macbeth, Richard, even Iago,—we think not so much of the crimes which they commit, as of the ambition, the aspiring spirit, the intellectual activity, which prompts them to overleap those moral fences. Barnwell is a wretched murderer; there is a certain fitness between his neck and the rope; he is the legitimate heir to the gallows; nobody who thinks at all can think of any alleviating circumstances in his case to make him a fit object of mercy. Or to take an instance from the higher tragedy, what else but a mere assassin is Glenalvon! Do we think of any thing but of the crime which he commits, and the rack which he deserves? That is all which we really think about him. Whereas in corresponding characters in Shakspeare so little do the actions comparatively affect us, that while the impulses, the inner mind in all its perverted greatness, solely seems real and is exclusively attended to, the crime is comparatively nothing. But when we see these things represented, the acts which they do are comparatively every thing, their impulses nothing. The state of sublime emotion into which we are elevated by those images of night and horror which Macbeth is made to utter, that solemn prelude with which he entertains the time till the bell shall strike which is to call him to murder Duncan,—when we no longer read it in a book, when we have given up that vantage-ground of abstraction which reading possesses over seeing, and come to see a man in his bodily shape before our eyes actually preparing to commit a murder, if the acting be true and impressive, as I have witnessed it in Mr K.'s performance of that part, the painful anxiety about the act, the natural longing to prevent it while it yet seems unperpetrated, the too close pressing semblance of reality, give a pain and an uneasiness which totally destroy all the delight which the words in the book convey, where the deed doing never presses upon us with the painful sense of presence: it rather seems to belong to history, —to something past and inevitable, if it has any thing to do with time at all. The sublime images, the poetry alone, is that which is present to our minds in the reading.

So to see Lear acted,—to see an old man tottering about the stage with a walking-stick, turned out of doors by his daughters in a rainy night, has nothing in it but what is painful and disgusting. We want to take him into shelter and relieve him. That is all the feeling which the acting of Lear ever produced in me. But the Lear of Shakspeare cannot be acted. The contemptible machinery by which they mimic the storm which he goes out in, is not more inadequate to represent the horrors of the real elements, than any actor can be to represent Lear: they might more easily propose to personate the Satan of Milton upon a stage, or one of Michael Angelo's terrible figures. The greatness of Lear is not in corporal dimension, but in intellectual: the explosions of his passion are terrible as a volcano: they are storms turning up and disclosing to the bottom that sea, his mind, with all its vast riches. It is his mind which is laid bare. This case of flesh and blood seems too insignificant to be thought on; even as he himself neglects it. On the stage we see nothing but corporal infirmities and weakness, the impotence of rage; while we read it, we see not Lear, but we are Lear,—we are in his mind, we are sustained by a grandeur which baffles the malice of daughters and storms; in the aberrations of his reason, we discover a mighty irregular power of reasoning, immethodized from the ordinary purposes of life, but exerting its powers, as the wind blows where it listeth, at will upon the corruptions and abuses of mankind. What have looks, or tones, to do with that sublime identification of his age with that of the *heavens themselves*, when in his reproaches to them for conniving at the injustice of his children, he reminds them that 'they themselves are old.' What gesture shall we appropriate to this? What has the voice or the eye to do with such things? But the play is beyond all art, as the tamperings with it shew: it is too hard and stony; it must have love-scenes, and a happy ending. It is not enough that Cordelia is a daughter, she must shine as a lover too. Tate has put his hook in the nostrils of this Leviathan, for Garrick and his followers, the showmen of the scene, to draw the mighty beast about more easily. A happy ending!—as if the living martyr-dom that Lear had gone through,—the flaying of his feelings alive, did not make a fair dismissal from the stage of life the only decorous thing for him. If he is to live and be happy after, if he could sustain this world's burden after, why all this pudder and preparation,—why torment us with all this unnecessary sympathy? As if the childish pleasure of getting his gilt robes and sceptre again could tempt him to act over again his misused station,—as if at his years, and with his experience, any thing was left but to die.

Lear is essentially impossible to be represented on a stage. But how many dramatic personages are there in Shakspeare, which though more tractable and feasible (if I may so speak) than Lear, yet from some circumstance, some adjunct to their character, are improper to be shewn to our bodily eye. Othello for instance. Nothing can be more soothing, more flattering to the nobler parts of our natures, than to read of a young Venetian lady of highest extraction, through the force of love and from a sense of merit in him whom she loved, laying aside every consideration of kindred, and country, and colour, and wedding with *a coal-black Moor*—(for such he is represented, in the imperfect state of knowledge respecting foreign countries in those days, compared with our own, or in compliance with popular notions, though the Moors are now well enough known to be by many shades less unworthy of a white woman's fancy)

—it is the perfect triumph of virtue over accidents, of the imagination over the senses. She sees Othello's colour in his mind. But upon the stage, when the imagination is no longer the ruling faculty, but we are left to our poor unassisted senses, I appeal to every one that has seen Othello played, whether he did not, on the contrary, sink Othello's mind in his colour; whether he did not find something extremely revolting in the courtship and wedded caresses of Othello and Desdemona; and whether the actual sight of the thing did not over-weigh all that beautiful compromise which we make in reading;— and the reason it should do so is obvious, because there is just so much reality presented to our senses as to give a perception of disagreement, with not enough of belief in the internal motives,—all that which is unseen,—to overpower and recon- cile the first and obvious prejudices[1]. What we see upon a stage is body and bodily action; what we are conscious of in reading is almost exclusively the mind, and its movements: and this I think may sufficiently account for the very different sort of delight with which the same play so often affects us in the reading and the seeing.

It requires little reflection to perceive, that if those characters in Shakspeare which are within the precincts of nature, have yet something in them which appeals too exclusively to the imagination, to admit of their being made objects to the senses without suffering a change and a diminution,—that still stronger the objection must lie against representing another line of characters, which Shakspeare has introduced to give a wildness and a supernatural elevation to his scenes, as if to remove them still farther from that assimilation to common life in which their excellence is vulgarly supposed to consist. When we read the incantations of those terrible beings the Witches in Mac- beth, though some of the ingredients of their hellish composition

---

[1] The error of supposing that because Othello's colour does not offend us in the reading, it should also not offend us in the seeing, is just such a fallacy as supposing that an Adam and Eve in a picture shall affect us just as they do in the poem. But in the poem we for a while have Paradisaical senses given us, which vanish when we see a man and his wife without clothes in the picture. The painters them- selves feel this, as is apparent by the awkward shifts they have recourse to, to make them look not quite naked; by a sort of prophetic ana- chronism, antedating the invention of fig-leaves. So in the reading of the play, we see with Desdemona's eyes; in the seeing of it, we are forced to look with our own.

savour of the grotesque, yet is the effect upon us other than the most serious and appalling that can be imagined? Do we not feel spell-bound as Macbeth was? Can any mirth accompany a sense of their presence? We might as well laugh under a consciousness of the principle of Evil himself being truly and really present with us. But attempt to bring these beings on to a stage, and you turn them instantly into so many old women, that men and children are to laugh at. Contrary to the old saying, that 'seeing is believing,' the sight actually destroys the faith; and the mirth in which we indulge at their expense, when we see these creatures upon a stage, seems to be a sort of indemnification which we make to ourselves for the terror which they put us in when reading made them an object of belief,—when we surrendered up our reason to the poet, as children to their nurses and their elders; and we laugh at our fears, as children who thought they saw something in the dark, triumph when the bringing in of a candle discovers the vanity of their fears. For this exposure of supernatural agents upon a stage is truly bringing in a candle to expose their own delusiveness. It is the solitary taper and the book that generates a faith in these terrors: a ghost by chandelier light, and in good company, deceives no spectators,—a ghost that can be measured by the eye, and his human dimensions made out at leisure. The sight of a well-lighted house, and a well-dressed audience, shall arm the most nervous child against any apprehensions: as Tom Brown says of the impenetrable skin of Achilles with his impenetrable armour over it, 'Bully Dawson would have fought the devil with such advantages.'

Much has been said, and deservedly, in reprobation of the vile mixture which Dryden has thrown into the Tempest: doubtless without some such vicious alloy, the impure ears of that age would never have sate out to hear so much innocence of love as is contained in the sweet courtship of Ferdinand and Miranda. But is the Tempest of Shakspeare at all a subject for stage representation? It is one thing to read of an enchanter, and to believe the wondrous tale while we are reading it; but to have a conjuror brought before us in his conjuring-gown, with his spirits about him, which none but himself and some hundred of favoured spectators before the curtain are supposed to see, involves such a quantity of the *hateful incredible*, that all our reverence for the author cannot hinder us from perceiving such gross attempts upon the senses to be in the highest degree childish and inefficient. Spirits and fairies cannot be represented, they cannot even be painted,—they can only be believed. But the elaborate and anxious provision of scenery, which the luxury of the age demands, in these cases works a quite contrary effect to what is intended. That which in comedy, or plays of familiar life, adds so much to the life of the imitation, in plays which appeal to the higher faculties, positively destroys the illusion which it is introduced to aid. A parlour or a drawing-room,—a library opening into a garden, —a garden with an alcove in it,—a street, or the piazza of Covent-garden, does well enough in a scene; we are content to give as much credit to it as it demands; or rather, we think little about it,—it is little more than reading at the top of a page, 'Scene, a Garden'; we do not imagine ourselves there, but we readily admit the imitation of familiar objects. But to think by the help of painted trees and caverns, which we know to be painted, to transport our minds to Prospero, and his island and his lonely cell[1]; or by the aid of a fiddle dexterously thrown in, in an interval of speaking, to make us believe that we hear those supernatural noises of which the isle was full:— the Orrery Lecturer at the Haymarket might as well hope, by his musical glasses cleverly stationed out of sight behind his apparatus, to make us believe that we do indeed hear the chrystal spheres ring out that chime, which if it were to inwrap our fancy long, Milton thinks,

> Time would run back and fetch the age of gold,
> And speckled vanity
> Would sicken soon and die,
> And leprous Sin would melt from earthly mould;
> Yea Hell itself would pass away,
> And leave its dolorous mansions to the peering day.

The Garden of Eden, with our first parents in it, is not more impossible to be shewn on a stage, than the Enchanted Isle, with its no less interesting and innocent first settlers.

The subject of Scenery is closely connected with that of the Dresses, which are so anxiously attended to on our stage. I remember the last time I saw Macbeth played, the discrepancy I felt at the changes of garment which he varied,—the shiftings

[1] It will be said these things are done in pictures. But pictures and scenes are very different things. Painting is a world of itself, but in scene-painting there is the attempt to deceive; and there is the discordancy, never to be got over, between painted scenes and real people.

and re-shiftings, like a Romish priest at mass. The luxury of stage-improvements, and the importunity of the public eye, require this. The coronation robe of the Scottish monarch was fairly a counterpart to that which our King wears when he goes to the Parliament-house,—just so full and cumbersome, and set out with ermine and pearls. And if things must be represented, I see not what to find fault with in this. But in reading, what robe are we conscious of? Some dim images of royalty—a crown and sceptre, may float before our eyes, but who shall describe the fashion of it? Do we see in our mind's eye what Webb or any other robe-maker could pattern? This is the inevitable consequence of imitating every thing, to make all things natural. Whereas the reading of a tragedy is a fine abstraction. It presents to the fancy just so much of external appearances as to make us feel that we are among flesh and blood, while by far the greater and better part of our imagination is employed upon the thoughts and internal machinery of the character. But in acting, scenery, dress, the most contemptible things, call upon us to judge of their naturalness.

Perhaps it would be no bad similitude, to liken the pleasure which we take in seeing one of these fine plays acted, compared with that quiet delight which we find in the reading of it, to the different feelings with which a reviewer, and a man that is not a reviewer, reads a fine poem. The accursed critical habit, —the being called upon to judge and pronounce, must make it quite a different thing to the former. In seeing these plays acted, we are affected just as judges. When Hamlet compares the two pictures of Gertrude's first and second husband, who wants to see the pictures? But in the acting, a miniature must be lugged out; which we know not to be the picture, but only to shew how finely a miniature may be represented. This shewing of every thing, levels all things: it makes tricks, bows, and curtesies, of importance. Mrs S. never got more fame by any thing than by the manner in which she dismisses the guests in the banquet-scene in Macbeth: it is as much remembered as any of her thrilling tones or impressive looks. But does such a trifle as this enter into the imaginations of the readers of that wild and wonderful scene? Does not the mind dismiss the feasters as rapidly as it can? Does it care about the gracefulness of the doing it? But by acting, and judging of acting, all these non-essentials are raised into an importance, injurious to the main interest of the play.

I have confined my observations to the tragic parts of Shakspeare. It would be no very difficult task to extend the enquiry to his comedies; and to shew why Falstaff, Shallow, Sir Hugh Evans, and the rest, are equally incompatible with stage representation. The length to which this Essay has run, will make it, I am afraid, sufficiently distasteful to the Amateurs of the Theatre, without going any deeper into the subject at present.

The Reflector. 1811.

SHAKSPEARE, *RICHARD III*

I am possessed with an admiration of the genuine Richard, his genius, and his mounting spirit, which no consideration of his cruelties can depress. Shakspeare has not made Richard so black a Monster as is supposed. Wherever he is monstrous, it was to conform to vulgar opinion. But he is generally a Man. Read his most exquisite address to the Widowed Queen to court her daughter for him—the topics of maternal feeling, of a deep knowledge of the heart, are such as no monster could have supplied. Richard must have *felt* before he could feign so well; tho' ambition choked the good seed. I think it the most finished piece of Eloquence in the world; of *persuasive* oratory far above Demosthenes, Burke, or any man, far exceeding the courtship of Lady Anne. *Her* relenting is barely natural, after all; the more perhaps S.'s merit to make *impossible* appear *probable*, but the *Queen's consent* (taking in all the circumstances and topics, *private* and *public*, with his angelic address, able to draw the host of [piece cut out of letter] Lucifer) is *probable*; and [piece cut out of letter] resisted it. This observation applies to many other parts. All the inconsistency is, that Shakspeare's better genius was forced to struggle against the prejudices which made a monster of Richard. He set out to paint a *monster*, but his human sympathies produced a *man*.

Letter to Robert Lloyd, July 26, 1801.

We are ready to acknowledge, that this Actor presents us with a very original and very forcible portrait (if not of the *man Richard*, whom Shakspeare drew, yet) of the *monster Richard*, as he exists in the *popular idea*, in *his own exaggerated* and *witty self-abuse*, in the overstrained representations of the

4—2

parties who were *sufferers* by his *ambition*; and, above all, in the impertinent and wretched *scenes*, so absurdly foisted in by some, who have thought themselves capable of adding to what *Shakespeare wrote*.

But of Mr Cooke's *Richard*:

1st. *His predominant and masterly simulation.*

He has a tongue can wheedle with the DEVIL.

It has been the policy of that antient and grey simulator, in all ages, to hide his *horns* and *claws*. The *Richard* of Mr Cooke perpetually obtrudes *his*. We see the effect of his deceit uniformly *successful*, but we do not comprehend *how it succeeds*. We can put ourselves, by a very common fiction, into the place of the individuals upon whom it acts, and say, that, in the like case, we should not have been alike credulous. The hypocrisy is too glaring and visible. It resembles more the shallow cunning of a mind which is its own dupe, than the profound and practised art of so powerful an intellect as *Richard's*. It is too obstreperous and loud, breaking out into *triumphs* and *plaudits* at its own success, like an unexercised *noviciate* in *tricks*. It has none of the silent confidence, and steady self-command of the *experienced politician*; it possesses none of that *fine address*, which was necessary to have betrayed the heart of *Lady Anne*, or even to have imposed upon the duller wits of the *Lord Mayor* and *Citizens*.

2dly. *His habitual jocularity*, the effect of buoyant spirits, and an elastic mind, rejoicing in its own powers, and in the success of its machinations. This quality of unstrained mirth accompanies *Richard*, and is a prime feature in his character. It never leaves him; in plots, in stratagems, and in the midst of his bloody devices, it is perpetually driving him upon wit, and jests, and personal satire, fanciful allusions, and quaint felicities of phrase. It is one of the chief artifices by which the consummate master of dramatic effect has contrived to soften the horrors of the scene, and to make us contemplate a bloody and vicious character with delight. No where, in any of his plays, is to be found so much of sprightly colloquial dialogue, and soliloquies of genuine humour, as in *Richard*. This character of unlaboured mirth Mr Cooke seems entirely to pass over, and substitutes in its stead the coarse, taunting humour, and clumsy merriment, of a low-minded assassin.

3dly. *His personal deformity.*—When the *Richard* of Mr Cooke makes allusions to his own *form*, they seem accompanied with *unmixed distaste* and *pain*, like some obtrusive and *haunting* idea—But surely the *Richard* of Shakspeare mingles in these allusions a perpetual reference to his own powers and capacities, by which he is enabled to surmount these petty objections; and the joy of a defect *conquered*, or *turned* into an advantage, is one cause of these very allusions, and of the satisfaction, with which his mind recurs to them. These allusions themselves are made in an ironical and good humoured spirit of exaggeration—the most bitter of them are to be found in his self-congratulating soliloquy spoken in the very moment and crisis of joyful exultation on the success of his unheard of courtship.

G. F. Cooke in Richard III. 1802.

SHAKSPEARE, *TWELFTH NIGHT*

Malvolio is not essentially ludicrous. He becomes comic but by accident. He is cold, austere, repelling; but dignified, consistent, and, for what appears, rather of an over-stretched morality. Maria describes him as a sort of Puritan; and he might have worn his gold chain with honour in one of our old round-head families, in the service of a Lambert, or a Lady Fairfax. But his morality and his manners are misplaced in Illyria. He is opposed to the proper *levities* of the piece, and falls in the unequal contest. Still his pride, or his gravity, (call it which you will) is inherent, and native to the man, not mock or affected, which latter only are the fit objects to excite laughter. His quality is at the best unlovely, but neither buffoon nor contemptible. His bearing is lofty, a little above his station, but probably not much above his deserts. We see no reason why he should not have been brave, honourable, accomplished. His careless committal of the ring to the ground (which he was commissioned to restore to Cesario), bespeaks a generosity of birth and feeling[1]. His dialect on all occasions is that of a gentleman, and a man of education. We must not confound him with the eternal old, low steward of comedy. He is master of the household to a great Princess; a dignity

[1] *Viola.* She took the ring from me; I'll none of it.
     Mal. Come, Sir, you peevishly threw it to her; and her will is, it should be so returned. If it be worth stooping for, there it lies in your eye; if not, be it his that finds it.

probably conferred upon him for other respects than age or length of service[1]. Olivia, at the first indication of his supposed madness, declares that she 'would not have him miscarry for half of her dowry.' Does this look as if the character was meant to appear little or insignificant? Once, indeed, she accuses him to his face—of what?—of being 'sick of self-love,' —but with a gentleness and considerateness which could not have been, if she had not thought that this particular infirmity shaded some virtues. His rebuke to the knight, and his sottish revellers, is sensible and spirited; and when we take into consideration the unprotected condition of his mistress, and the strict regard with which her state of real or dissembled mourning would draw the eyes of the world upon her house-affairs, Malvolio might feel the honour of the family in some sort in his keeping; as it appears not that Olivia had any more brothers, or kinsmen, to look to it—for Sir Toby had dropped all such nice respects at the buttery hatch. That Malvolio was meant to be represented as possessing estimable qualities, the expression of the Duke in his anxiety to have him reconciled, almost infers. 'Pursue him, and entreat him to a peace.' Even" in his abused state of chains and darkness, a sort of greatness seems never to desert him. He argues highly and well with the supposed Sir Topas, and philosophises gallantly upon his straw[2]. There must have been some shadow of worth about the man; he must have been something more than a mere vapour—a thing of straw, or Jack in office—before Fabian and Maria could have ventured sending him upon a courting-errand to Olivia. There was some consonancy (as he would say) in the undertaking, or the jest would have been too bold even for that house of misrule.

[1] Mrs Inchbald seems to have fallen into the common mistake of the character in some sensible observations, otherwise, upon this Comedy. 'It might be asked,' she says, 'whether this credulous steward was much deceived in imputing a degraded taste, in the sentiments of love, to his fair lady Olivia, as she actually did fall in love with a domestic; and one, who from his extreme youth, was perhaps a greater reproach to her discretion, than had she cast a tender regard upon her old and faithful servant.' But where does she gather the fact of his age? Neither Maria nor Fabian ever cast that reproach upon him.

[2] *Clown.* What is the opinion of Pythagoras concerning wild fowl?
Mal. That the soul of our grandam might haply inhabit a bird.
Clown. What thinkest thou of his opinion?
Mal. I think nobly of the soul, and no way approve of his opinion.

Bensley, accordingly, threw over the part an air of Spanish
loftiness. He looked, spake, and moved like an old Castilian.
He was starch, spruce, opinionated, but his superstructure of
pride seemed bottomed upon a sense of worth. There was
something in it beyond the coxcomb. It was big and swelling,
but you could not be sure that it was hollow. You might wish
to see it taken down, but you felt that it was upon an elevation.
He was magnificent from the outset; but when the decent
sobrieties of the character began to give way, and the poison
of self-love, in his conceit of the Countess's affection, gradually
to work, you would have thought that the hero of La Mancha
in person stood before you. How he went smiling to himself!
with what ineffable carelessness would he twirl his gold chain!
what a dream it was! you were infected with the illusion, and
did not wish that it should be removed! you had no room for
laughter! if an unseasonable reflection of morality obtruded
itself, it was a deep sense of the pitiable infirmity of man's
nature, that can lay him open to such frenzies—but in truth
you rather admired than pitied the lunacy while it lasted—you
felt that an hour of such mistake was worth an age with the
eyes open. Who would not wish to live but for a day in the
conceit of such a lady's love as Olivia? Why, the Duke would
have given his principality but for a quarter of a minute,
sleeping or waking, to have been so deluded. The man seemed
to tread upon air, to taste manna, to walk with his head in the
clouds, to mate Hyperion. O! shake not the castles of his
pride—endure yet for a season, bright moments of confidence
—'stand still ye watches of the element,' that Malvolio may
be still in fancy fair Olivia's lord—but fate and retribution say
no—I hear the mischievous titter of Maria—the witty taunts of
Sir Toby—the still more insupportable triumph of the foolish
knight—the counterfeit Sir Topas is unmasked—and 'thus
the whirligig of time,' as the true clown hath it, 'brings in his
revenges.' I confess that I never saw the catastrophe of this character, while Bensley played it, without a kind of tragic interest.

On Some of the Old Actors, in *The Essays of Elia*. 1822.

SHAKSPEARE, *OTHELLO*

[Bensley's]Iago was the only endurable one which I remember
to have seen. No spectator from his action could divine more of
his artifice than Othello was supposed to do. His confessions

in soliloquy alone put you in possession of the mystery. There were no by-intimations to make the audience fancy their own discernment so much greater than that of the Moor—who commonly stands like a great helpless mark set up for mine Ancient, and a quantity of barren spectators, to shoot their bolts at. The Iago of Bensley did not go to work so grossly. There was a triumphant tone about the character, natural to a general consciousness of power; but none of that petty vanity which chuckles and cannot contain itself upon any little successful stroke of its knavery—as is common with your small villains, and green probationers in mischief. It did not clap or crow before its time. It was not a man setting his wits at a child, and winking all the while at other children who are mightily pleased at being let into the secret; but a consummate villain entrapping a noble nature into toils, against which no discernment was available, where the manner was as fathomless as the purpose seemed dark, and without motive.

On Some of the Old Actors, in *The Essays of Elia*. 1822.

KING LEAR, THE NUT-BROWN MAID, MATTHEW PRIOR AND *THE BALLAD OF FAIR ROSAMUND*

> *Lear.* Who are you?
> Mine eyes are not o' the best: I'll tell you straight.
> ...Are you not Kent?
> *Kent.* The same;
> Your servant Kent. Where is your servant Caius?
> *Lear.* He's a good fellow, I can tell you that;
> He'll strike, and quickly too; he's dead and rotten.
> *Kent.* No, my good Lord; I am the very man—
> *Lear.* I'll see that straight—
> *Kent.* That from your first of difference and decay,
> Have follow'd your sad steps.
> *Lear.* You are welcome hither....
> *Albany.* He knows not what he says; and vain it is
> That we present us to him.
> *Edgar.* Look up, my Lord.
> *Kent.* Vex not his ghost. O, let him pass! He hates him
> That would upon the rack of this tough world
> Stretch him out longer.

So ends 'King Lear,' the most stupendous of the Shakspearian dramas; and Kent, the noblest feature of the conceptions of his divine mind. This is the magnanimity of authorship, when a writer, having a topic presented to him, fruitful of beauties for common minds, waives his privilege, and trusts to the judicious few for understanding the reason of his abstinence. What a pudder would a common dramatist have raised here of a reconciliation scene, a perfect recognition, between the assumed Caius and his master!—to the suffusing of many fair eyes, and the moistening of cambric handkerchiefs. The old dying king partially catching at the truth, and immediately lapsing into obliviousness, with the high-minded carelessness of the other to have his services appreciated, as one that

> —served not for gain,
> Or follow'd out of form,

are among the most judicious, not to say heart-touching, strokes in Shakspeare.

Allied to this magnanimity it is, where the pith and point of an argument, the amplification of which might compromise the modesty of the speaker, is delivered briefly, and, as it were, *parenthetically*; as in those few but pregnant words, in which the man in the old 'Nut-brown Maid' rather intimates than reveals his unsuspected high birth to the woman:—

> Now understand, to Westmorland,
> *Which is my heritage,*
> I will you bring, and with a ring,
> By way of marriage,
> I will you take, and Lady make.

Turn we to the version of it, ten times diluted, of dear Mat. Prior—in his own way unequalled, and a poet now-a-days too much neglected—'In me,' quoth Henry, addressing the astounded Emma—with a flourish and an attitude, as we may conceive:—

> In me behold the potent Edgar's heir,
> Illustrious Earl! him terrible in war,
> Let Loire confess.

And with a deal of skimble-skamble stuff, as Hotspur would term it, more, presents the Lady with a full and true enumeration of his Papa's rent-roll in the fat soil by Deva.

But of all parentheses, (not to quit the topic too suddenly) commend me to that most significant one, at the commencement of the old popular ballad of Fair Rosamund:—

> When good King Henry ruled this land,
> The second of that name,

Now mark—

> (Besides the Queen) he dearly loved
> A fair and comely dame.

There is great virtue in this *besides*.

Table-Talk by the late Elia, in *The Athenaeum*. 1834.

HENRY PORTER, *THE TWO ANGRY WOMEN OF ABINGDON*

This pleasant comedy is contemporary with some of the earliest of Shakspeare's, and is no wit inferior to either the *Comedy of Errors*, or the *Taming of the Shrew*, for instance. It is full of business, humour, and merry malice. Its night-scenes are peculiarly sprightly and wakeful. The versification unencumbered, and rich with compound epithets.

Notes, etc., to Extracts from the Garrick Plays. 1827.

JOHN DAY, *THE PARLIAMENT OF BEES*

Whether this singular production, in which the characters are all *Bees*, was ever acted, I have no information to determine. It is at least as capable of representation as we can conceive the 'Birds' of Aristophanes to have been.

> [*Ulania, a female Bee, speaks:*] Philon, a Bee
> Well-skilled in verse and amorous poetry,
> As we have sate at work, both of one Rose,
> Has humm'd sweet canzons, both in verse and prose,
> Which I ne'er minded.

Prettily pilfered from the sweet passage in the *Midsummer Night's Dream*, where Helena recounts to Hermia their school-days' friendship:—

> We, Hermia, like two artificial gods,
> Created with our needles both one flower,
> Both on one sampler, sitting on one cushion.

> —The doings,
> The births, the wars, the wooings,

of these pretty little winged creatures are with continued liveliness portrayed throughout the whole of this curious old drama, in words which bees would talk with, could they talk; the very air seems replete with humming and buzzing melodies, while we read them. Surely bees were never so be-rhymed before.

Notes, etc., to Extracts from the Garrick Plays. 1827.

MASSINGER

Massinger had not the higher requisites of his art in any thing like the degree in which they were possessed by Ford, Webster, Tourneur, Heywood, and others. He never shakes or disturbs the mind with grief. He is read with composure and placid delight. He wrote with that equability of all the passions, which made his English style the purest and most free from violent metaphors and harsh constructions, of any of the dramatists who were his contemporaries.

Notes to Specimens of Dramatic Poets who lived about the Time of Shakspeare. 1808.

THOMAS HEYWOOD

If I were to be consulted as to a Reprint of our old English Dramatists, I should advise to begin with the collected Plays of Heywood. He was a fellow Actor, and fellow Dramatist, with Shakspeare. He possessed not the imagination of the latter; but in all those qualities which gained for Shakspeare the attribute of *gentle*, he was not inferior to him. Generosity, courtesy, temperance in the depths of passion; sweetness, in a word, and gentleness; Christianism; and true hearty Anglicism of feelings, shaping that Christianism; shine throughout his beautiful writings in a manner more conspicuous than in those of Shakspeare, but only more conspicuous, inasmuch as in Heywood these qualities are primary, in the other subordinate to poetry. I love them both equally, but Shakspeare has most of my wonder. Heywood should be known to his countrymen, as he deserves. His plots are almost invariably English. I am sometimes jealous, that Shakspeare laid so few of his scenes at home. I laud Ben Jonson, for that in one instance having framed the first draught of his *Every Man in his Humour* in Italy, he changed the scene, and Anglicised his characters.

Notes, etc., to Extracts from the Garrick Plays. 1827.

CERVANTES, *DON QUIXOTE*

Deeply corporealised, and enchained hopelessly in the grovelling fetters of externality, must be the mind, to which, in its better moments, the image of the high-souled, highintelligenced Quixote—the errant Star of Knighthood, made more tender by eclipse—has never presented itself, divested from the unhallowed accompaniment of a Sancho, or a rabble-ment at the heels of Rosinante. That man has read his book by halves; he has laughed, mistaking his author's purport, which was—tears. The artist that pictures Quixote (and it is in this degrading point that he is every season held up at our Exhibitions) in the shallow hope of exciting mirth, would have joined the rabble at the heels of his starved steed. We wish not to see *that* counterfeited, which we would not have wished to see in the reality. Conscious of the heroic insight of the noble Quixote, who, on hearing that his withered person was passing, would have stepped over his threshold to gaze upon his forlorn habiliments, and the 'strange bed-fellows which misery brings a man acquainted with'? Shade of Cervantes! who in thy Second Part could put into the mouth of thy Quixote those high aspirations of a super-chivalrous gallantry, where he replies to one of the shepherdesses, apprehensive that he would spoil their pretty net-works, and inviting him to be a guest with them, in accents like these: 'Truly, fairest Lady, Actæon was not more astonished when he saw Diana bathing herself at the fountain, than I have been in beholding your beauty: I commend the manner of your pastime, and thank you for your kind offers; and, if I may serve you, so I may be sure you will be obeyed, you may command me: for my profession is this, To show myself thankful, and a doer of good to all sorts of people, especially of the rank that your person shows you to be; and if those nets, as they take up but a little piece of ground, should take up the whole world, I would seek out new worlds to pass through, rather than break them: and (he adds,) that you may give credit to this my exaggeration, behold at least he that promiseth you this, is Don Quixote de la Mancha, if haply this name hath come to your hearing.' Illustrious Romancer! were the 'fine frenzies,' which possessed the brain of thy own Quixote, a fit subject, as in this second Part, to be exposed to the jeers of Duennas and Serving Men? to be monstered, and shown up at the heartless banquets of great men? Was that pitiable infirmity, which in thy First Part misleads him, *always from within*, into half-ludicrous, but more than half-compassionable and admir-able errors, not infliction enough from heaven, that men by studied artifices must devise and practise upon the humour, to

inflame where they should soothe it? Why, Goneril would
have blushed to practise upon the abdicated king at this rate,
and the she-wolf Regan not have endured to play the pranks
upon his fled wits, which thou hast made thy Quixote suffer
in Duchesses' halls, and at the hands of that unworthy nobleman[1].

In the First Adventures, even, it needed all the art of the
most consummate artist in the Book way that the world hath
yet seen, to keep up in the mind of the reader the heroic
attributes of the character without relaxing; so as absolutely
that they shall suffer no alloy from the debasing fellowship of
the clown. If it ever obtrudes itself as a disharmony, are we
inclined to laugh; or not, rather, to indulge a contrary emotion?
—Cervantes, stung, perchance, by the relish with which *his*
Reading Public had received the fooleries of the man, more to
their palates than the generosities of the master, in the sequel
let his pen run riot, lost the harmony and the balance, and
sacrificed a great idea to the taste of his contemporaries. We
know that in the present day the Knight has fewer admirers
than the Squire. Anticipating, what did actually happen to
him—as afterwards it did to his scarce inferior follower, the
Author of 'Guzman de Alfarache'—that some less knowing
hand would prevent him by a spurious Second Part: and
judging, that it would be easier for his competitor to out-bid
him in the comicalities, than in the *romance*, of his work, he
abandoned his Knight, and has fairly set up the Squire for his
Hero. For what else has he unsealed the eyes of Sancho; and
instead of that twilight state of semi-insanity—the madness at
second-hand—the contagion, caught from a stronger mind infected—that war between native cunning, and hereditary defer-
ence, with which he has hitherto accompanied his master—
two for a pair almost—does he substitute a downright Knave,
with open eyes, for his own ends only following a confessed
Madman; and offering at one time to lay, if not actually laying,
hands upon him! From the moment that Sancho loses his
reverence, Don Quixote is become a—treatable lunatic. Our
artists handle him accordingly.

*Barrenness of the Imaginative Faculty in the Produc-
tions of Modern Art*, in *The Last Essays of Elia*. 1831.

---

[1] Yet from this Second Part, our cried-up pictures are mostly
selected; the waiting-women with beards, etc.

ON THE POETICAL WORKS OF GEORGE WITHER

The poems of G. Wither are distinguished by a hearty homeliness of manner, and a plain moral speaking. He seems to have passed his life in one continued act of an innocent self-pleasing. That which he calls his *Motto* is a continued self-eulogy of two thousand lines, yet we read it to the end without any feeling of distaste, almost without a consciousness that we have been listening all the while to a man praising himself. There are none of the cold particles in it, the hardness and self-ends which render vanity and egotism hateful. He seems to be praising another person, under the mask of self; or rather we feel that it was indifferent to him where he found the virtue which he celebrates; whether another's bosom, or his own, were its chosen receptacle. His poems are full, and this in particular is one downright confession, of a generous self-seeking. But by self he sometimes means a great deal,— his friends, his principles, his country, the human race.

Whoever expects to find in the satirical pieces of this writer any of those peculiarities which pleased him in the satires of Dryden or Pope, will be grievously disappointed. Here are no high-finished characters, no nice traits of individual nature, few or no personalities. The game run down is coarse general vice, or folly as it appears in classes. A liar, a drunkard, a coxcomb, is *stript and whipt*; no Shaftesbury, no Villiers, or Wharton, is curiously anatomized, and read upon. But to a well-natured mind there is a charm of moral sensibility running through them which amply compensates the want of those luxuries. Wither seems every where bursting with a love of goodness and a hatred of all low and base actions.—At this day it is hard to discover what parts in the poem here particularly alluded to, *Abuses Stript and Whipt*, could have occasioned the imprisonment of the author. Was Vice in High Places more suspicious than now? had she more power; or more leisure to listen after ill reports? That a man should be convicted of a libel when he named no names but Hate, and Envy, and Lust, and Avarice, is like one of the indictments in the *Pilgrim's Progress*, where Faithful is arraigned for having 'railed on our noble Prince Beelzebub, and spoken contemptibly of his honourable friends, the Lord Old Man, the Lord Carnal Delight, and the Lord Luxurious.' What unlucky jealousy could have tempted the great men of those days to appropriate such innocent abstractions to themselves!

Wither seems to have contemplated to a degree of idolatry his own possible virtue. He is for ever anticipating persecution and martyrdom; fingering, as it were, the flames, to try how he can bear them. Perhaps his premature defiance sometimes made him obnoxious to censures, which he would otherwise have slipped by.

The homely versification of these Satires is not likely to attract in the present day. It is certainly not such as we should expect from a poet 'soaring in the high region of his fancies with his garland and his singing robes about him'[1]; nor is it such as he has shown in his *Philarete*, and in some parts in his *Shepherds Hunting*. He seems to have adopted this dress with voluntary humility, as fittest for a moral teacher, as our divines chuse sober grey or black; but in their humility consists their sweetness. The deepest tone of moral feeling in them, (though all throughout is weighty, earnest and passionate) is in those pathetic injunctions against shedding of blood in quarrels, in the chapter entitled *Revenge*. The story of his own forbearance, which follows, is highly interesting. While the Christian sings his own victory over Anger, the Man of Courage cannot help peeping out to let you know, that it was some higher principle than *fear* which counselled his forbearance.

Whether encaged, or roaming at liberty, Wither never seems to have abated a jot of that free spirit, which sets its mark upon his writings, as much as a predominant feature of independence impresses every page of our late glorious Burns; but the elder poet wraps his proof-armour closer about him, the other wears his too much outwards; he is thinking too much of annoying the foe, to be quite easy within; the spiritual defences of Wither are a perpetual source of inward sunshine, the magnanimity of the modern is not without its alloy of soreness, and a sense of injustice, which seems perpetually to gall and irritate. Wither was better skilled in the 'sweet uses of adversity,' he knew how to extract the 'precious jewel' from the head of the 'toad,' without drawing any of the 'ugly venom' along with it.—The prison notes of Wither are finer than the wood notes of most of his poetical brethren. The description in the Fourth Eglogue of his *Shepherds Hunting* (which was composed during his imprisonment in the Marshal-

[1] Milton.

sea) of the power of the Muse to extract pleasure from common
objects, has been oftener quoted, and is more known, than any
part of his writings. Indeed the whole Eglogue is in a strain
so much above not only what himself, but almost what any
other poet has written, that he himself could not help noticing
it; he remarks, that his spirits had been raised higher than
they were wont 'through the love of poesy.'—The praises of
Poetry have been often sung in ancient and in modern times;
strange powers have been ascribed to it of influence over
animate and inanimate auditors; its force over fascinated
crowds has been acknowledged; but, before Wither, no one
ever celebrated its power *at home*, the wealth and the strength
which this divine gift confers upon its possessor. Fame, and
that too after death, was all which hitherto the poets had
promised themselves from their art. It seems to have been
left to Wither to discover, that poetry was a present possession,
as well as a rich reversion, and that the Muse had promise of
both lives, of this, and of that which was to come.

The *Mistress of Philarete* is in substance a panegyric pro-
tracted through several thousand lines in the mouth of a single
speaker, but diversified, so as to produce an almost dramatic
effect, by the artful introduction of some ladies, who are rather
auditors than interlocutors in the scene; and of a boy, whose
singing furnishes pretence for an occasional change of metre:
though the seven syllable line, in which the main part of it is
written, is that in which Wither has shown himself so great a
master, that I do not know that I am always thankful to him
for the exchange.

Wither has chosen to bestow upon the lady whom he com-
mends, the name of Arete, or Virtue; and assuming to himself
the character of Philarete, or Lover of Virtue, there is a sort
of propriety in that heaped measure of perfections, which he
attributes to this partly real, partly allegorical, personage.
Drayton before him had shadowed his mistress under the
name of Idea, or Perfect Pattern, and some of the old Italian
love-strains are couched in such religious terms as to make it
doubtful, whether it be a mistress, or Divine Grace, which the
poet is addressing.

In this poem (full of beauties) there are two passages of
pre-eminent merit. The first is where the lover, after a flight
of rapturous commendation, expresses his wonder why all men
that are about his mistress, even to her very servants, do not
view her with the same eyes that he does.

Sometime I do admire,
All men burn not with desire;
Nay I muse her servants are not
Pleading love; but O! they dare not.
And I therefore wonder, why
They do not grow sick and die.
Sure they would do so, but that,
By the ordinance of fate,
There is some concealed thing
So each gazer limiting,
He can see no more of merit
Than beseems his worth and spirit,
For in her a grace there shines,
That o'er-daring thoughts confines;
Making worthless men despair
To be lov'd of one so fair.
Yea the destinies agree,
Some *good judgments* blind should be,
And not gain the power of knowing
Those rare beauties in her growing.
Reason doth as much imply:
For if every judging eye,
Which beholdeth her, should there
Find what excellencies are;
All, o'ercome by those perfections,
Would be captive to affections.
So, in happiness unblest,
She for lovers should not rest.

The other is, where he has been comparing her beauties to gold, and stars, and the most excellent things in nature; and, fearing to be accused of hyperbole, the common charge against poets, vindicates himself by boldly taking upon him, that these comparisons are no hyperboles; but that the best things in nature do, in a lover's eye, fall short of those excellencies which he adores in her.

What pearls, what rubies can
Seem so lovely fair to man,
As her lips whom he doth love,
When in sweet discourse they move,
Or her lovelier teeth, the while
She doth bless him with a smile?
Stars indeed fair creatures be;
Yet amongst us where is he
Joys not more the whilst he lies
Sunning in his mistress' eyes,
Than in all the glimmering light
Of a starry winter's night?
Note the beauty of an eye—
And if aught you praise it by

Leave such passion in your mind,
Let my reason's eye be blind.
Mark if ever red or white
Any where gave such delight,
As when they have taken place
In a worthy woman's face.

.   .   .   .

I must praise her as I may,
Which I do mine own rude way;
Sometime setting forth her glories
By unheard-of allegories—etc.

To the measure in which these lines are written, the wits of
Queen Anne's days contemptuously gave the name of Namby
Pamby, in ridicule of Ambrose Philips, who had used it in
some instances, as in the lines on Cuzzoni, to my feeling at
least, very deliciously; but Wither, whose darling measure it
seems to have been, may shew, that in skilful hands it is capable
of expressing the subtilest movements of passion. So true it
is, which Drayton seems to have felt, that it is the poet who
modifies the metre, not the metre the poet; in his own words,
that

It's possible to climb;
To kindle, or to slake;
Altho' in Skelton's rhime[1].

---

[1] A long line is a line we are long repeating. In the *Shepherds
Hunting* take the following—

If thy verse doth bravely tower,
As she makes wing, she gets power;
Yet the higher she doth soar,
She's affronted still the more,
'Till she to the high'st hath past,
Then she rests with fame at last.

What longer measure can go beyond the majesty of this! What
Alexandrine is half so long in pronouncing, or expresses *labor slowly
but strongly surmounting difficulty* with the life with which it is done
in the second of these lines? or what metre could go beyond these
from *Philarete*—

Her true beauty leaves behind
Apprehensions in my mind
Of more sweetness, than all art
Or inventions can impart.
Thoughts too deep to be express'd,
And too strong to be suppress'd.

From the *Works* of 1818.

WITHER AND QUARLES

I perfectly accord with your opinion of old Wither; Quarles is a wittier writer, but Wither lays more hold of the heart. Quarles thinks of his audience when he lectures; Wither soliloquizes in company from a full heart. What wretched stuff are the 'Divine Fancies' of Quarles! Religion appears to him no longer valuable than it furnishes matters for quibbles and riddles; he turns God's grace into wantonness. Wither is like an old friend, whose warm-heartedness and estimable qualities make us wish he possessed more genius, but at the same time make us willing to dispense with that want. I always love Wither, and sometimes ádmire Quarles. Still that portrait poem is a fine one; and the extract from 'Shepherds' Hunting' places him in a starry height far above Quarles.

Letter to Southey, Nov. 8, 1798.

WALTON, *THE COMPLETE ANGLER*

I shall expect you to bring me a brimful account of the pleasure which Walton has given you, when you come to town. It must square with your mind. The delightful innocence and healthfulness of the Angler's mind will have blown upon yours like a Zephyr. Don't you already feel your spirit *filled* with the scenes?—the banks of rívers—the cowslip beds—the pastoral scenes—the neat alehouses—and hostesses and milkmaids, as far exceeding Virgil and Pope, as the *Holy Living* is beyond Thomas à Kempis. Are not the eating and drinking joys painted to the Life? Do they not inspire you with an immortal hunger? Are not you ambitious of being made an Angler?... The *Complete Angler* is the only Treatise written in Dialogues that is worth a halfpenny. Many elegant dialogues have been written (such as Bishop Berkeley's *Minute Philosopher*), but in all of them the Interlocutors are merely abstract arguments personify'd; not living dramatic characters, as in Walton, where *every thing* is *alive*; the fishes are absolutely *charactered*; and birds and animals are as interesting as men and women.

Letter to Robert Lloyd, Feb. 7, 1801.

SIR THOMAS BROWNE

'I have read of a bird, which hath a face like, and yet will prey upon, a man; who coming to the water to drink, and finding there by reflection, that he had killed one like himself, pineth away by degrees, and never afterwards enjoyeth itself.' I do not know where Fuller read of this bird; but a more awful and affecting story, and moralizing of a story, in Natural History, or rather in that Fabulous Natural History, where poets and mythologists found the Phœnix and the Unicorn, and 'other strange fowl,' is no where extant. It is a fable which Sir Thomas Browne, if he had heard of it, would have exploded among his Vulgar Errors; but the delight which he would have taken in the discussing of its probabilities, would have shewn that the *truth of the fact*, though the avowed object of his search, was not so much the motive which put him upon the investigation, as those hidden affinities and poetical analogies,—those *essential verities* in the application of strange fable, which made him linger with such reluctant delay among the last fading lights of popular tradition; and not seldom to conjure up a superstition, that had been long extinct, from its dusty grave, to inter it himself with greater ceremonies and solemnities of burial.

Specimens from the Writings of
Fuller, the Church Historian. 1811.

The beautiful obliquities of the Religio Medici.

Mackery End, in Hertfordshire,
in *The Essays of Elia.* 1821.

MILTON'S LATIN PROSE WORKS

The first Defence is the greatest work among them, because it is uniformly great, and such as is befitting the very mouth of a great nation, speaking for itself. But the second Defence, which is but a succession of splendid episodes, slightly tied together, has one passage, which, if you have not read, I conjure you to lose no time, but read it: it is his consolations in his blindness, which had been made a reproach to him. It begins whimsically, with poetical flourishes about Tiresias and other blind worthies, (which still are mainly interesting as dis-

playing his singular mind, and in what degree poetry entered
into his daily soul, not by fits and impulses, but engrained and
innate,) but the concluding page, *i.e.* of *this passage*, (not of
the *Defensio*,) which you will easily find, divested of all brags
and flourishes, gives so rational, so true an enumeration of
his comforts, so human, that it cannot be read without the
deepest interest.

Letter to Coleridge, Nov. 4, 1802.

MILTON, *PARADISE REGAINED*

The severest satire upon full tables and surfeits is the banquet
which Satan, in the Paradise Regained, provides for a temptation in the wilderness:

> A table richly spread in regal mode,
> With dishes piled, and meats of noblest sort
> And savour; beasts of chase, or fowl of game,
> In pastry built, or from the spit, or boiled,
> Gris-amber-steamed; all fish from sea or shore,
> Freshet or purling brook, for which was drained
> Pontus, and Lucrine bay, and Afric coast.

The Tempter, I warrant you, thought these cates would go
down without the recommendatory preface of a benediction.
They are like to be short graces where the devil plays the host.
—I am afraid the poet wants his usual decorum in this place.
Was he thinking of the old Roman luxury, or of a gaudy day
at Cambridge? This was a temptation fitter for a Heliogabalus.
The whole banquet is too civic and culinary, and the accom-
paniments altogether a profanation of that deep, abstracted,
holy scene. The mighty artillery of sauces, which the cook-
fiend conjures up, is out of proportion to the simple wants and
plain hunger of the guest. He that disturbed him in his dreams,
from his dreams might have been taught better. To the temperate fantasies of the famished Son of God, what sort of
feasts presented themselves?—He dreamed indeed,

> —As appetite is wont to dream,
> Of meats and drinks, nature's refreshment sweet.

But what meats:—

> Him thought, he by the brook of Cherith stood,
> And saw the ravens with their horny beaks
> Food to Elijah bringing, even and morn;
> Though ravenous, taught to abstain from what they brought:
> He saw the prophet also how he fled
> Into the desert, and how there he slept

Under a juniper; then how awaked
He found his supper on the coals prepared,
And by the angel was bid rise and eat,
And ate the second time after repose,
The strength whereof sufficed him forty days:
Sometimes, that with Elijah he partook,
Or as a guest with Daniel at his pulse.

Nothing in Milton is finelier fancied than these temperate
dreams of the divine Hungerer. To which of these two visionary
banquets, think you, would the introduction of what is called
the grace have been most fitting and pertinent?

Grace before Meat, in *The Essays of Elia*. 1821.

FULLER

The writings of Fuller are usually designated by the title of
quaint, and with sufficient reason; for such was his natural
bias to conceits, that I doubt not upon most occasions it would
have been going out of his way to have expressed himself out
of them. But his wit is not always a *lumen siccum*, a dry faculty
of surprising; on the contrary, his conceits are oftentimes
deeply steeped in human feeling and passion. Above all, his
way of telling a story, for its eager liveliness, and the perpetual
running commentary of the narrator happily blended with the
narration, is perhaps unequalled.

'St Paul saith, let not the sun go down on your wrath, to
carry news to the antipodes in another world of thy revengeful
nature. Yet let us take the Apostle's meaning rather than his
words, with all possible speed to depose our passion; not
understanding him so literally, that we may take leave to be
angry till sunset: then might our wrath lengthen with the
days; and men in Greenland, where the day lasts above a
quarter of a year, have plentiful scope for revenge.'

This whimsical prevention of a consequence which no one
would have thought of deducing,—setting up an absurdum on
purpose to hunt it down,—placing guards as it were at the
very outposts of possibility,—gravely giving out laws to insanity
and prescribing moral fences to distempered intellects, could
never have entered into a head less entertainingly constructed
than that of Fuller, or Sir Thomas Browne, the very air of
whose style the conclusion of this passage most aptly imitates.

Henry de Essex.—'He is too well known in our English
Chronicles, being Baron of Raleigh, in Essex, and Hereditary
Standard Bearer of England. It happened in the reign of this
king [Henry II] there was a fierce battle fought in Flintshire,
at Coleshall, between the English and Welsh, wherein this
Henry de Essex *animum et signum simul abjecit*, betwixt traitor
and coward, cast away both his courage and banner together,
occasioning a great overthrow of English. But he that had the
baseness to do, had the boldness to deny the doing of so foul a
fact; until he was challenged in combat by Robert de Momford,
a knight, eye-witness thereof, and by him overcome in a duel.
Whereupon his large inheritance was confiscated to the king,
and he himself, *partly thrust, partly going into a convent, hid
his head in a cowl, under which, betwixt shame and sanctity, he
blushed out the remainder of his life.*'—Worthies. Article, Bed-
fordshire.

The fine imagination of Fuller has done what might have
been pronounced impossible: it has given an interest, and a
holy character, to coward infamy. Nothing can be more beautiful than the concluding account of the last days, and expiatory
retirement, of poor Henry de Essex. The address with which
the whole of this little story is told is most consummate: the
charm of it seems to consist in a perpetual balance of antitheses
not too violently opposed, and the consequent activity of mind
in which the reader is kept:—'Betwixt traitor and coward'—
'baseness to do, boldness to deny'—'partly thrust, partly going,
into a convent'—'betwixt shame and sanctity.' The reader by
this artifice is taken into a kind of partnership with the writer,
—his judgment is exercised in settling the preponderance,—he
feels as if he were consulted as to the issue. But the modern
historian flings at once the dead weight of his own judgment
into the scale, and settles the matter.

*Specimens from the Writings of
Fuller, the Church Historian.* 1811.

JEREMY TAYLOR

If you are yet but lightly acquainted with his real manner,
take up and read the whole first chapter of the Holy DYING;
in particular turn to the first paragraph of the second section

of that chapter for a simile of a rose, or more truly many similes within simile; for such were the riches of his fancy, that when a beauteous image offered, before he could stay to expand it into all its capacities, throngs of new coming images came up, and justled out the first, or blended in disorder with it, which imitates the order of every rapid mind. But read all the first chapter by my advice; and I know I need not advise you, when you have read it, to read the second.

Or for another specimen (where so many beauties crowd, the judgment has yet vanity enough to think it can discern a handsomest, till a second judgment and a third *ad infinitum* start up to disallow their elder brother's pretensions) turn to the story of the Ephesian Matron in the second section of the 5th chapter of the same Holy DYING (I still refer to the *Dying* part, because it contains better matter than the 'Holy Living,' which deals more in rules than illustrations—I mean in comparison with the other only, else it has more and more beautiful illustrations—than any prose book besides)—read it yourself and show it to Plumstead (with my LOVE, and bid him write to me), and ask him if WILLY himself has ever told a story with more circumstances of FANCY and HUMOUR.

The paragraph begins, 'But that which is to be faulted,' and the story not long after follows. Make these references while P. is with you, that you may stir him up to the LOVE of Jeremy Taylor, and make a convertite of him. Coleridge was the man who first solemnly exhorted me to 'study' the works of Dr Jeremy Taylor, and I have had reason to bless the hour in which he did it. Read as many of his works as you can get. I will assist you in getting them when we go a stall hunting together in London, and it's odds if we don't get a good Beaumt. and Fletcher cheap.

Bp. Taylor has more and more beautiful imagery, and (what is more to a Lover of Willy) more knowledge and description of human life and manners than any prose book in the language: he has more delicacy and sweetness than any mortal, the 'gentle' Shakspeare hardly excepted,—his similes and allusions are taken, as the bees take honey, from all the youngest, greenest, exquisitest parts of nature, from plants, and flowers, and fruit, young boys and virgins, from little children perpetually, from sucking infants, babies' smiles, roses, gardens, —his imagination was a spacious Garden, where no vile insects could crawl in; his apprehension a 'COURT' where no foul thoughts kept 'leets and holy-days.'

> Snail and worm, give no offence,
> Newt nor blind worm be not seen,
> Come not near our fairy queen.

You must read Bishop Taylor with allowances for the subjects on which he wrote, and the age *in* which. You may skip or patiently endure his tedious discourses on rites and ceremonies, Baptism, and the Eucharist, the Clerical function, and the antiquity of Episcopacy, a good deal of which are inserted in works not purely controversial; his polemical works you may skip altogether, unless you have a taste for the exertions of vigorous reason and subtle distinguishing on uninteresting topics. Such of his works as you should begin with, to get a taste for him (after which your Love will lead you to his Polemical and drier works, as Love led Leander 'over boots' knee-deep thro' the Hellespont), but read first the *Holy Living and Dying*, and his *Life of Christ* and *Sermons*, both in folio. And, above all, try to get a beautiful little tract on the 'Measures and offices of Friendship,' printed with his *opuscula* duodecimo, and also at the end of his Polemical Discourses in folio. Another thing you will observe in Bp. Taylor, without which consideration you will do him injustice. He wrote to different classes of people. His *Holy Living and Dying* and *Life of Christ* were designed and have been used as popular books of family Devotion, and have been thumbed by old women, and laid about in the window seats of old houses in great families, like the Bible, and the 'Queene-like-Closet or rare boke of Recipes in medicine and cookery, fitted to all capacities.'

Accordingly in these *the fancy* is perpetually applied to; any slight conceit, allusion, or analogy, any 'prettiness,' a story true or false, serves for an argument adapted to women and young persons, and 'incompetent judgments'; whereas the *Liberty of Prophecy* (a book in your father's bookcase) is a series of severe and masterly reasoning, fitted to great Clerks and learned Fathers, with no more of Fancy than is subordinate and ornamental.—Such various powers had the Bishop of Down and Connor, Administrator of the See of Dromore!

My theme and my story!—Farewell.

Letter to Robert Lloyd, April 6, 1801.

RESTORATION COMEDY

The artificial Comedy, or Comedy of manners, is quite extinct on our stage. Congreve and Farquhar show their heads once in seven years only, to be exploded and put down instantly. The times cannot bear them. Is it for a few wild speeches, an occasional license of dialogue? I think not altogether. The business of their dramatic characters will not stand the moral test. We screw every thing up to that. Idle gallantry in a fiction, a dream, the passing pageant of an evening, startles us in the same way as the alarming indications of profligacy in a son or ward in real life should startle a parent or guardian. We have no such middle emotions as dramatic interests left. We see a stage libertine playing his loose pranks of two hours' duration, and of no after consequence, with the severe eyes which inspect real vices with their bearings upon two worlds. We are spectators to a plot or intrigue (not reducible in life to the point of strict morality) and take it all for truth. We substitute a real for a dramatic person, and judge him accordingly. We try him in our courts, from which there is no appeal to the *dramatis personæ*, his peers. We have been spoiled with —not sentimental comedy—but a tyrant far more pernicious to our pleasures which has succeeded to it, the exclusive and all devouring drama of common life; where the moral point is every thing; where, instead of the fictitious half-believed personages of the stage (the phantoms of old comedy) we recognise ourselves, our brothers, aunts, kinsfolk, allies, patrons, enemies, —the same as in life,—with an interest in what is going on so hearty and substantial, that we cannot afford our moral judgment, in its deepest and most vital results, to compromise or slumber for a moment. What is *there* transacting, by no modification is made to affect us in any other manner than the same events or characters would do in our relationships of life. We carry our fire-side concerns to the theatre with us. We do not go thither, like our ancestors, to escape from the pressure of reality, so much as to confirm our experience of it; to make assurance double, and take a bond of fate. We must live our toilsome lives twice over, as it was the mournful privilege of Ulysses to descend twice to the shades. All that neutral ground of character, which stood between vice and virtue; or which in fact was indifferent to neither, where neither properly was called in question; that happy breathing-place from the

burthen of a perpetual moral questioning—the sanctuary and
quiet Alsatia of hunted casuistry—is broken up and dis-
franchised, as injurious to the interests of society. The privileges of the place are taken away by law. We dare not dally
with images, or names, of wrong. We bark like foolish dogs
at shadows. We dread infection from the scenic representation
of disorder; and fear a painted pustule. In our anxiety that
our morality should not take cold, we wrap it up in a great
blanket surtout of precaution against the breeze of sunshine.

I confess for myself that (with no great delinquencies to
answer for) I am glad for a season to take an airing beyond the
diocese of the strict conscience,—not to live always in the
precincts of the law-courts,—but now and then, for a dream-
while or so, to imagine a world with no meddling restrictions
—to get into recesses, whither the hunter cannot follow me—

> —Secret shades
> Of woody Ida's inmost grove,
> While yet there was no fear of Jove—

I come back to my cage and my restraint the fresher and more
healthy for it. I wear my shackles more contentedly for having
respired the breath of an imaginary freedom. I do not know
how it is with others, but I feel the better always for the
perusal of one of Congreve's—nay, why should I not add even
of Wycherley's—comedies. I am the gayer at least for it; and
I could never connect those sports of a witty fancy in any
shape with any result to be drawn from them to imitation in
real life. They are a world of themselves almost as much as
fairy-land. Take one of their characters, male or female (with
few exceptions they are alike), and place it in a modern play,
and my virtuous indignation shall rise against the profligate
wretch as warmly as the Catos of the pit could desire; because
in a modern play I am to judge of the right and the wrong.
The standard of *police* is the measure of *political justice*. The
atmosphere will blight it, it cannot live here. It has got into
a moral world, where it has no business, from which it must
needs fall headlong; as dizzy, and incapable of making a stand,
as a Swedenborgian bad spirit that has wandered unawares
into the sphere of one of his Good Men, or Angels. But in its
own world do we feel the creature is so very bad?—The Fainalls
and the Mirabels, the Dorimants and the Lady Touchwoods,
in their own sphere, do not offend my moral sense; in fact
they do not appeal to it at all. They seem engaged in their

proper element. They break through no laws, or conscientious restraints. They know of none. They have got out of Christendom into the land—what shall I call it?—of cuckoldry—the Utopia of gallantry, where pleasure is duty, and the manners perfect freedom. It is altogether a speculative scene of things, which has no reference whatever to the world that is. No good person can be justly offended as a spectator, because no good person suffers on the stage. Judged morally, every character in these plays—the few exceptions only are *mistakes*—is alike essentially vain and worthless. The great art of Congreve is especially shown in this, that he has entirely excluded from his scenes,—some little generosities in the part of Angelica perhaps excepted,—not only any thing like a faultless character, but any pretensions to goodness or good feelings whatsoever. Whether he did this designedly, or instinctively, the effect is as happy, as the design (if design) was bold. I used to wonder at the strange power which his Way of the World in particular possesses of interesting you all along in the pursuits of characters, for whom you absolutely care nothing—for you neither hate nor love his personages—and I think it is owing to this very indifference for any, that you endure the whole. He has spread a privation of moral light, I will call it, rather than by the ugly name of palpable darkness, over his creations; and his shadows flit before you without distinction or preference. Had he introduced a good character, a single gush of moral feeling, a revulsion of the judgment to actual life and actual duties, the impertinent Goshen would have only lighted to the discovery of deformities, which now are none, because we think them none.

Translated into real life, the characters of his, and his friend Wycherley's dramas, are profligates and strumpets,—the business of their brief existence, the undivided pursuit of lawless gallantry. No other spring of action, or possible motive of conduct, is recognised; principles which, universally acted upon, must reduce this frame of things to a chaos. But we do them wrong in so translating them. No such effects are produced in *their* world. When we are among them, we are amongst a chaotic people. We are not to judge them by our usages. No reverend institutions are insulted by their proceedings,—for they have none among them. No peace of families is violated,—for no family ties exist among them. No purity of the marriage bed is stained,—for none is supposed to have a being. No deep affections are disquieted,—no holy wedlock bands are snapped asunder,—for affection's depth and wedded faith are not of the growth of that soil. There is neither right nor wrong,—gratitude or its opposite,—claim or duty,—paternity or sonship. Of what consequence is it to virtue, or how is she at all concerned about it, whether Sir Simon, or Dapperwit, steal away Miss Martha; or who is the father of Lord Froth's, or Sir Paul Pliant's children.

The whole is a passing pageant, where we should sit as unconcerned at the issues, for life or death, as at a battle of the frogs and mice. But, like Don Quixote, we take part against the puppets, and quite as impertinently. We dare not contemplate an Atlantis, a scheme, out of which our coxcombical moral sense is for a little transitory ease excluded. We have not the courage to imagine a state of things for which there is neither reward nor punishment. We cling to the painful necessities of shame and blame. We would indict our very dreams.

On the Artificial Comedy of the Last Century, in *The Essays of Elia*. 1822.

THE GENTEEL STYLE IN WRITING

It is an ordinary criticism, that my Lord Shaftesbury, and Sir William Temple, are models of the genteel style in writing. We should prefer saying—of the lordly, and the gentlemanly. Nothing can be more unlike than the inflated finical rhapsodies of Shaftesbury, and the plain natural chit-chat of Temple. The man of rank is discernible in both writers; but in the one it is only insinuated gracefully, in the other it stands out offensively. The peer seems to have written with his coronet on, and his Earl's mantle before him; the commoner in his elbow chair and undress.—What can be more pleasant than the way in which the retired statesman peeps out in the essays, penned by the latter in his delightful retreat at Shene? They scent of Nimeguen, and the Hague. Scarce an authority is quoted under an ambassador. Don Francisco de Melo, a 'Portugal Envoy in England,' tells him it was frequent in his country for men, spent with age or other decays, so as they could not hope for above a year or two of life, to ship themselves away in a Brazil fleet, and after their arrival there to go on a great

length, sometimes of twenty or thirty years, or more, by the
force of that vigour they recovered with that remove. 'Whether
such an effect (Temple beautifully adds) might grow from the
air, or the fruits of that climate, or by approaching nearer the
sun, which is the fountain of light and heat, when their natural
heat was so far decayed: or whether the piecing out of an old
man's life were worth the pains; I cannot tell: perhaps the
play is not worth the candle.'—Monsieur Pompone, 'French
Ambassador in his (Sir William's) time at the Hague,' certifies
him, that in his life he had never heard of any man in France
that arrived at a hundred years of age; a limitation of life
which the old gentleman imputes to the excellence of their
climate, giving them such a liveliness of temper and humour,
as disposes them to more pleasures of all kinds than in other
countries; and moralises upon the matter very sensibly. The
'late Robert Earl of Leicester' furnishes him with a story of
a Countess of Desmond, married out of England in Edward
the Fourth's time, and who lived far in King James's reign.
The 'same noble person' gives him an account, how such a
year, in the same reign, there went about the country a set of
morrice-dancers, composed of ten men who danced, a Maid
Marian, and a tabor and pipe; and how these twelve, one with
another, made up twelve hundred years. 'It was not so much
(says Temple) that so many in one small county (Hereford-
shire) should live to that age, as that they should be in vigour
and in humour to travel and to dance.' Monsieur Zulichem,
one of his 'colleagues at the Hague,' informs him of a cure
for the gout; which is confirmed by another 'Envoy,' Monsieur
Serinchamps in that town, who had tried it.—Old Prince
Maurice of Nassau recommends to him the use of hammocks
in that complaint; having been allured to sleep, while suffering
under it himself, by the 'constant motion or swinging of those
airy beds.' Count Egmont, and the Rainegrave who 'was
killed last summer before Maestricht,' impart to him their
experiences.

But the rank of the writer is never more innocently disclosed,
than where he takes for granted the compliments paid by
foreigners to his fruit-trees. For the taste and perfection of
what we esteem the best, he can truly say, that the French,
who have eaten his peaches and grapes at Shene in no very
ill year, have generally concluded that the last are as good as
any they have eaten in France on this side Fontainebleau; and

the first as good as any they have eat in Gascony. Italians have agreed his white figs to be as good as any of that sort in Italy, which is the earlier kind of white fig there; for in the later kind and the blue, we cannot come near the warm climates, no more than in the Frontignac or Muscat grape. His orange-trees, too, are as large as any he saw when he was young in France, except those of Fontainebleau, or what he has seen since in the Low Countries; except some very old ones of the Prince of Orange's. Of grapes he had the honour of bringing over four sorts into England, which he enumerates, and sup-poses that they are all by this time pretty common among some gardeners in his neighbourhood, as well as several persons of quality; for he ever thought all things of this kind 'the commoner they are made the better.' The garden pedantry with which he asserts that 'tis to little purpose to plant any of the best fruits, as peaches or grapes, hardly, he doubts, beyond Northamptonshire at the furthest northwards; and praises the 'Bishop of Munster at Cosevelt,' for attempting nothing beyond cherries in that cold climate; is equally pleasant and in character. 'I may perhaps' (he thus ends his sweet Garden Essay with a passage worthy of Cowley) 'be allowed to know something of this trade, since I have so long allowed myself to be good for nothing else, which few men will do, or enjoy their gardens, without often looking abroad to see how other matters play, what motions in the state, and what invitations they may hope for into other scenes. For my own part, as the country life, and this part of it more particularly, were the inclination of my youth itself so they are the pleasure of my age; and I can truly say that, among many great em-ployments that have fallen to my share, I have never asked or sought for any of them, but have often endeavoured to escape from them, into the ease and freedom of a private scene, where a man may go his own way and his own pace, in the common paths and circles of life. The measure of choosing well is whether a man likes what he has chosen, which I thank God has befallen on me; and though among the follies of my life, building and planting have not been the least, and have cost me more than I have the confidence to own; yet they have been fully recompensed by the sweetness and satisfaction of this retreat, where, since my resolution taken of never entering again into any public employments, I have passed five years without ever once going to town, though I am almost in sight of it, and have a house there always ready to receive me. Nor has this been any sort of affectation, as some have thought it, but a mere want of desire or humour to make so small a remove; for when I am in this corner, I can truly say with Horace, *Me quoties reficit, etc.*

> 'Me, when the cold Digentian stream revives,
> What does my friend believe I think or ask?
> Let me yet less possess, so I may live,
> Whate'er of life remains, unto myself.
> May I have books enough; and one year's store,
> Not to depend upon each doubtful hour:
> This is enough of mighty Jove to pray,
> Who, as he pleases, gives and takes away.'

The writings of Temple are, in general, after this easy copy. On one occasion, indeed, his wit, which was mostly subordinate to nature and tenderness, has seduced him into a string of felicitous antitheses; which, it is obvious to remark, have been a model to Addison and succeeding essayists. 'Who would not be covetous, and with reason,' he says, 'if health could be purchased with gold? Who not ambitious, if it were at the command of power, or restored by honour? but, alas! a white staff will not help gouty feet to walk better than a common cane; nor a blue riband bind up a wound so well as a fillet. The glitter of gold, or of diamonds, will but hurt sore eyes instead of curing them; and an aching head will be no more eased by wearing a crown, than a common night-cap.' In a far better style, and more accordant with his own humour of plainness, are the concluding sentences of his 'Discourse upon Poetry.' Temple took a part in the controversy about the ancient and the modern learning; and, with that partiality so natural and so graceful in an old man, whose state engagements had left him little leisure to look into modern productions, while his retirement gave him occasion to look back upon the classic studies of his youth—decided in favour of the latter. 'Certain it is,' he says, 'that, whether the fierceness of the Gothic humours, or noise of their perpetual wars, frighted it away, or that the unequal mixture of the modern languages would not bear it—the great heights and excellency both of poetry and music fell with the Roman learning and empire, and have never since recovered the admiration and applauses that before attended them. Yet, such as they are amongst us, they must be confessed to be the softest and sweetest, the most general and most innocent amusements of common time and life. They still find room in the courts of princes, and the cottages of shepherds. They serve to revive and animate the dead calm of poor and idle lives, and to allay or divert the violent passions and perturbations of the greatest and the busiest men. And both these effects are of equal use to human life; for the mind of man is like the sea, which is neither agreeable to the beholder nor the voyager, in a calm or in a storm, but is so to both when a little agitated by gentle gales; and so the mind, when moved by soft and easy passions or affections. I know very well that many who pretend to be wise by the forms of being grave, are apt to despise both poetry and music, as toys and trifles too light for the use or entertainment of serious men. But whoever find themselves wholly insensible to their charms, would, I think, do well to keep their own counsel, for fear of reproaching their own temper, and bringing the goodness of their natures, if not of their understandings, into question. While this world lasts I doubt not but the pleasure and request of these two entertainments will do so too; and happy those that content themselves with these, or any other so easy and so innocent, and do not trouble the world or other men, because they cannot be quiet themselves, though nobody hurts them.' 'When all is done (he concludes), human life is at the greatest and the best but like a froward child, that must be played with, and humoured a little, to keep it quiet, till it falls asleep, and then the care is over.'

The Last Essays of Elia. 1826.

BURNET'S *HISTORY OF HIS OWN TIMES*

I am reading *Burnet's History of his own Times*. Did you ever read that garrulous, pleasant history? He tells his story like an old man past political service, bragging to his sons on winter evenings of the part he took in public transactions when his 'old cap was new.' Full of scandal, which all true history is. No palliatives; but all the stark wickedness, that actually gives the *momentum* to national actors. Quite the prattle of age, and outlived importance. Truth and sincerity staring out upon you perpetually in *alto relievo*. Himself a party man— he makes you a party man. None of the cursed philosophical Humeian indifference, so cold, and unnatural, and inhuman!

None of the cursed Gibbonian fine writing, so fine and com-
posite! None of Dr Robertson's periods with three members.
None of Mr Roscoe's sage remarks, all so apposite, and coming
in so clever, lest the reader should have had the trouble of
drawing an inference. Burnet's good old prattle I can bring
present to my mind; I can make the revolution present to me:
the French revolution, by a converse perversity in my nature,
I fling as far *from* me.

Letter to Manning, March 1, 1800.

ESTIMATE OF DE FOE'S SECONDARY NOVELS, 1830

It has happened not seldom that one work of some author
has so transcendantly surpassed in execution the rest of his
compositions, that the world has agreed to pass a sentence of
dismissal upon the latter, and to consign them to total neglect
and oblivion. It has done wisely in this, not to suffer the
contemplation of excellencies of a lower standard to abate, or
stand in the way of, the pleasure it has agreed to receive from
the master-piece.

Again it has happened, that from no inferior merit of execution in the rest, but from superior good fortune in the choice
of its subject, some single work shall have been suffered to
eclipse, and cast into shade the deserts of its less fortunate
brethren. This has been done with more or less injustice in
the case of the popular allegory of Bunyan, in which the
beautiful and scriptural image of a pilgrim or wayfarer (we
are all such upon earth), addressing itself intelligibly and
feelingly to the bosoms of all, has silenced, and made almost
to be forgotten, the more awful and scarcely less tender
beauties of the 'Holy War made by Shaddai upon Diabolus,'
of the same author; a romance less happy in its subject, but
surely well worthy of a secondary immortality. But in no
instance has this excluding partiality been exerted with more
unfairness than against what may be termed the secondary
novels or romances of De Foe.

While all ages and descriptions of people hang delighted
over the 'Adventures of Robinson Crusoe,' and shall continue
to do so we trust while the world lasts, how few comparatively
will bear to be told, that there exist other fictitious narratives
by the same writer—four of them at least of no inferior interest,

except what results from a less felicitous choice of situation. Roxana—Singleton—Moll Flanders—Colonel Jack—are all genuine offspring of the same father. They bear the veritable impress of De Foe. An unpractised midwife that would not swear to the nose, lip, forehead, and eye, of every one of them! They are in their way as full of incident, and some of them every bit as romantic; only they want the uninhabited Island, and the charm, that has bewitched the world, of the striking solitary situation.

But are there no solitudes out of the cave and the desert? or cannot the heart in the midst of crowds feel frightfully alone? Singleton, on the world of waters, prowling about with pirates less merciful than the creatures of any howling wilderness; is he not alone, with the faces of men about him, but without a guide that can conduct him through the mists of educational and habitual ignorance; or a fellow-heart that can interpret to him the new-born yearnings and aspirations of unpractised penitence? Or when the boy Colonel Jack, in the loneliness of the heart (the worst solitude), goes to hide his ill-purchased treasure in the hollow tree by night, and miraculously loses, and miraculously finds it again—whom hath he there to sympathise with him? or of what sort are his associates?

The narrative manner of De Foe has a naturalness about it, beyond that of any other novel or romance writer. His fictions have all the air of true stories. It is impossible to believe, while you are reading them, that a real person is not narrating to you every where nothing but what really happened to himself. To this, the extreme *homeliness* of their style mainly contributes. We use the word in its best and heartiest sense—that which comes *home* to the reader. The narrators everywhere are chosen from low life, or have had their origin in it; therefore they tell their own tales, (Mr Coleridge has anticipated us in this remark,) as persons in their degree are observed to do, with infinite repetition, and an overacted exactness, lest the hearer should not have minded, or have forgotten, some things that had been told before. Hence the emphatic sentences marked in the good old (but deserted) Italic type; and hence, too, the frequent interposition of the reminding old colloquial parenthesis, 'I say'—'mind'—and the like, when the story-teller repeats what, to a practised reader, might appear to have been sufficiently insisted upon before: which made an ingenious critic observe, that his works, in this kind, were excellent

6—2

reading for the kitchen. And, in truth, the heroes and heroines
of De Foe, can never again hope to be popular with a much
higher class of readers, than that of the servant-maid or the
sailor. Crusoe keeps its rank only by tough prescription;
Singleton, the pirate—Colonel Jack, the thief—Moll Flanders,
both thief and harlot—Roxana, harlot and something worse—
would be startling ingredients in the bill of fare of modern
literary delicacies. But, then, what pirates, what thieves, and
what harlots, are *the thief*, *the harlot*, and *the pirate* of De Foe?
We would not hesitate to say, that in no other book of fiction,
where the lives of such characters are described, is guilt and
delinquency made less seductive, or the suffering made more
closely to follow the commission, or the penitence more earnest
or more bleeding, or the intervening flashes of religious visitation, upon the rude and uninstructed soul, more meltingly and
fearfully painted. They, in this, come near to the tenderness
of Bunyan; while the livelier pictures and incidents in them,
as in Hogarth or in Fielding, tend to diminish that 'fastidious-
ness to the concerns ànd pursuits of common life, which an
unrestrained passion for the ideal and the sentimental is in
danger of producing.'

From *Walter Wilson's Memoirs of the
Life and Times of Daniel de Foe.* 1830.

DE FOE'S NOVELS

In the appearance of *truth*, in all the incidents and conversations that occur in them, they exceed any works of fiction
I am acquainted with. It is perfect illusion. The *author* never
appears in these self-narratives, (for so they ought to be called,
or rather autobiographies,) but the *narrator* chains us down to
an implicit belief in every thing he says. There is all the minute
detail of a log-book in it. Dates are painfully pressed upon the
memory. Facts are repeated over and over in varying phases,
till you cannot choose but believe them. It is like reading
evidence given in a court of justice. So anxious the story-teller
seems that the truth should be clearly comprehended, that
when he has told us a matter of fact or a motive, in a line or
two farther down he *repeats* it, with his favourite figure of
speech, 'I say,' so and so, though he had made it abundantly
plain before. This is in imitation of the common people's way

of speaking, or rather of the way in which they are addressed by a master or mistress, who wishes to impress something upon their memories, and has a wonderful effect upon matter-of-fact readers. Indeed it is to such principally that he writes. His style is everywhere beautiful, but plain and *homely* Robinson Crusoe is delightful to all ranks and classes, but it is easy to see that it is written in phraseology peculiarly adapted to the lower conditions of readers; hence it is an especial favourite with seafaring men, poor boys, servant-maids, etc. His novels are capital kitchen-reading, while they are worthy, from their deep interest, to find a shelf in the libraries of the wealthiest and the most learned. His passion for *matter-of-fact narrative* sometimes betrayed him into a long relation of common incidents, which might happen to any man, and have no interest but the intense appearance of truth in them, to commend them. The whole latter half or two-thirds of 'Colonel Jack' is of this description. The beginning of 'Colonel Jack' is the most affecting natural picture of a young thief that was ever drawn. His losing the stolen money in the hollow of a tree, and finding it again when he was in despair, and then being in equal distress at not knowing how to dispose of it, and several similar touches in the early history of the Colonel, evince a deep knowledge of human nature; and putting out of question the superior *romantic* interest of the latter, in my mind very much exceed Crusoe. 'Roxana' (first edition) is the next in interest, though he left out the best part of it in subsequent editions from a foolish hypercriticism of his friend Southerne. But 'Moll Flanders,' the 'Account of the Plague,' etc., are all of one family, and have the same stamp of character.

Letter to Walter Wilson, Dec. 16, 1822.

COWPER

I have been reading 'The Task' with fresh delight. I am glad you love Cowper. I could forgive a man for not enjoying Milton; but I would not call that man my friend who should be offended with the 'divine chit-chat of Cowper.'

Letter to Coleridge, Dec. 5, 1796.

COWPER'S TRANSLATION OF HOMER

I find Cowper is a favourite with nobody. His injudicious use of the stately slow Miltonic verse in a subject so very different, has given a distaste. Nothing can be more unlike to my fancy than Homer and Milton. Homer is perfect prattle, tho' exquisite prattle, compared to the deep oracular voice of Milton. In Milton you love to stop, and saturate your mind with every great image or sentiment; in Homer you want to go on, to have more of his agreeable narrative. Cowper delays you as much, walking over a Bowling Green, as the other does, travelling over steep Alpine heights, where the labour enters into and makes a part of the pleasure.

Letter to Charles Lloyd the elder, July 31, 1809.

MRS BARBAULD AND BOOKS FOR CHILDREN

'Goody Two Shoes' is almost out of print. Mrs Barbauld's stuff has banished all the old classics of the nursery; and the shopman at Newberry's hardly deigned to reach them off an old exploded corner of a shelf, when Mary asked for them. Mrs Barbauld's, and Mrs Trimmer's nonsense lay in piles about. Knowledge insignificant and vapid as Mrs Barbauld's books convey, it seems, must come to a child in the *shape* of *knowledge*; and his empty noddle must be turned with conceit of his own powers when he has learnt that a horse is an animal, and Billy is better than a horse, and such like; instead of that beautiful interest in wild tales, which made the child a man, while all the time he suspected himself to be no bigger than a child. Science has succeeded to poetry no less in the little walks of children than with men. Is there no possibility of averting this sore evil? Think what you would have been now, if instead of being fed with tales and old wives' fables in childhood, you had been crammed with geography and natural history!

Letter to Coleridge, Oct. 23, 1802.

GOETHE'S *FAUST* AND MARLOWE'S *FAUSTUS*

I thoroughly agree with you as to 'The German Faust,' as far as I can do justice to it from an English translation. 'Tis a disagreeable canting tale of seduction, which has nothing to do with the spirit of Faustus—Curiosity. Was the dark secret to be explored to end in the seducing of a weak girl, which might have been accomplished by earthly agency? When Marlowe gives *his* Faustus a mistress, he flies him at Helen, flower of Greece, to be sure, and not at Miss Betsy, or Miss Sally Thoughtless.

> Cut is the branch that bore the goodly fruit,
> And wither'd is Apollo's laurel tree:
> Faustus is dead.

What a noble natural transition from metaphor to plain speaking! as if the figurative had flagged in description of such a loss, and was reduced to tell the fact simply.

Letter to W. H. Ainsworth, Dec. 9, 1823.

SHERIDAN, *THE SCHOOL FOR SCANDAL*

Amidst the mortifying circumstances attendant upon growing old, it is something to have seen the School for Scandal in its glory. This comedy grew out of Congreve and Wycherley, but gathered some allays of the sentimental comedy which followed theirs. It is impossible that it should be now *acted*, though it continues, at long intervals to be announced in the bills. Its hero, when Palmer played it at least, was Joseph Surface. When I remember the gay boldness, the graceful solemn plausibility, the measured step, the insinuating voice —to express it in a word—the downright *acted* villany of the part, so different from the pressure of conscious actual wickedness,—the hypocritical assumption of hypocrisy,—which made Jack so deservedly a favourite in that character, I must needs conclude the present generation of play-goers more virtuous than myself, or more dense. I freely confess that he divided the palm with me with his better brother; that, in fact, I liked him quite as well. Not but there are passages,—like that, for instance, where Joseph is made to refuse a pittance to a poor relation,—incongruities which Sheridan was forced upon by the attempt to join the artificial with the sentimental comedy, either of which must destroy the other—but over these obstructions Jack's manner floated him so lightly, that a refusal from him no more shocked you, than the easy compliance of Charles gave you in reality any pleasure; you got over the paltry question as quickly as you could, to get back into the regions of pure comedy, where no cold moral reigns. The highly artificial manner of Palmer in this character counteracted every disagreeable impression which you might have received from the contrast, supposing them real, between the two brothers. You did not believe in Joseph with the same faith with which you believed in Charles. The latter was a pleasant reality, the former a no less pleasant poetical foil to it. The comedy, I have said, is incongruous; a mixture of Congreve with sentimental incompatibilities: the gaiety upon the whole is buoyant; but it required the consummate art of Palmer to reconcile the discordant elements.

A player with Jack's talents, if we had one now, would not dare to do the part in the same manner. He would instinctively avoid every turn which might tend to unrealise, and so to make the character fascinating. He must take his cue from his spectators, who would expect a bad man and a good man as rigidly opposed to each other as the death-beds of those geniuses are contrasted in the prints, which I am sorry to say have disappeared from the windows of my old friend Carrington Bowles, of St Paul's Church-yard memory—(an exhibition as venerable as the adjacent cathedral, and almost coeval) of the bad and good man at the hour of death; where the ghastly apprehensions of the former,—and truly the grim phantom with his reality of a toasting fork is not to be despised,—so finely contrast with the meek complacent kissing of the rod,—taking it in like honey and butter,—with which the latter submits to the scythe of the gentle bleeder, Time, who wields his lancet with the apprehensive finger of a popular young ladies' surgeon. What flesh, like loving grass, would not covet to meet half-way the stroke of such a delicate mower?—John Palmer was twice an actor in this exquisite part. He was playing to you all the while that he was playing upon Sir Peter and his lady. You had the first intimation of a sentiment before it was on his lips. His altered voice was meant to you, and you were to suppose that his fictitious co-flutterers on the stage perceived nothing at all of it. What was it to you if that half-reality, the husband, was over-reached by the puppetry —or the thin thing (Lady Teazle's reputation) was persuaded it was dying of a plethory? The fortunes of Othello and Desdemona were not concerned in it. Poor Jack has past from the stage in good time, that he did not live to this our age of seriousness. The pleasant old Teazle *King*, too, is gone in good time. His manner would scarce have past current in our day. We must love or hate—acquit or condemn—censure or pity— exert our detestable coxcombry of moral judgment upon every thing. Joseph Surface, to go down now, must be a downright revolting villain—no compromise—his first appearance must shock and give horror—his specious plausibilities, which the pleasurable faculties of our fathers welcomed with such hearty greetings, knowing that no harm (dramatic harm even) could come, or was meant to come of them, must inspire a cold and killing aversion. Charles (the real canting person of the scene —for the hypocrisy of Joseph has its ulterior legitimate ends, but his brother's professions of a good heart centre in down- right self-satisfaction) must be *loved*, and Joseph *hated*. To balance one disagreeable reality with another, Sir Peter Teazle must be no longer the comic idea of a fretful old bachelor bridegroom, whose teasings (while King acted it) were evi- dently as much played off at you, as they were meant to con- cern any body on the stage,—he must be a real person, capable in law of sustaining an injury—a person towards whom duties are to be acknowledged—the genuine crim-con antagonist of the villainous seducer Joseph. To realise him more, his suffer- ings under his unfortunate match must have the downright pungency of life—must (or should) make you not mirthful but uncomfortable, just as the same predicament would move you in a neighbour or old friend. The delicious scenes which give the play its name and zest, must affect you in the same serious manner as if you heard the reputation of a dear female friend attacked in your real presence. Crabtree, and Sir Benjamin— those poor snakes that live but in the sunshine of your mirth —must be ripened by this hot-bed process of realization into asps or amphisbænas; and Mrs Candour—O! frightful! be- come a hooded serpent. Oh who that remembers Parsons and Dodd—the wasp and butterfly of the School for Scandal—in those two characters; and charming natural Miss Pope, the perfect gentlewoman as distinguished from the fine lady of comedy, in his latter part—would forego the true scenic delight —the escape from life—the oblivion of consequences—the holiday barring out of the pedant Reflection—those Saturnalia of two or three brief hours, well won from the world—to sit instead at one of our modern plays—to have his coward con- science (that forsooth must not be left for a moment) stimulated with perpetual appeals—dulled rather, and blunted, as a faculty without repose must be—and his moral vanity pampered with images of notional justice, notional beneficence, lives saved without the spectators' risk, and fortunes given away that cost the author nothing?

On the Artificial Comedy of the Last Century, in *The Essays of Elia*. 1822.

THE LYRICAL BALLADS SECOND 1800 EDITION

Thanks for your letter and present. I had already borrowed your second volume. What most pleases me is, 'The Song of Lucy,' *Simon's sickly daughter*, in 'The Sexton,' made me *cry*. Next to these are the description of these continuous echoes in the story of 'Joanna's Laugh,' where the mountains, and all the scenery absolutely seem alive; and that fine Shakspearian character of the 'happy man,' in the 'Brothers,'

> that creeps about the fields,
> Following his fancies by the hour, to bring
> Tears down his cheek, or solitary smiles
> Into his face, until the setting sun
> Write Fool upon his forehead!

I will mention one more—the delicate and curious feeling in the wish for the 'Cumberland Beggar,' that he may have about him the melody of birds, although he hear them not. Here the mind knowingly passes a fiction upon herself, first substituting her own feeling for the Beggar's, and in the same breath detecting the fallacy, will not part with the wish. The 'Poet's Epitaph' is disfigured, to my taste, by the common satire upon parsons and lawyers in the beginning, and the coarse epithet of 'pin-point,' in the sixth stanza. All the rest is eminently good, and your own. I will just add that it appears to me a fault in the 'Beggar,' that the instructions conveyed in it are too direct, and like a lecture: they don't slide into the mind of the reader while he is imagining no such matter. An intelligent reader finds a sort of insult in being told, 'I will teach you how to think upon this subject.' This fault, if I am right, is in a ten-thousandth worse degree to be found in Sterne, and in many novelists and modern poets, who continually put a sign-post up to show where you are to feel. They set out with assuming their readers to be stupid; very different from *Robinson Crusoe*, the *Vicar of Wakefield*, *Roderick Random*, and other beautiful, bare narratives. There is implied an unwritten compact between author and reader; 'I will tell you a story, and I suppose you will understand it.' Modern novels, *St Leons* and the like, are full of such flowers as these—'Let not my reader suppose,' 'Imagine, if you can, modest!' etc. I will here have done with praise and blame. I have written so much, only that you may not think I have passed over your book without observation....I am sorry that Coleridge has christened his *Ancient Marinere*, a *Poet's Reverie*; it is as bad as Bottom the Weaver's declaration that he is not a lion, but only the scenical representation of a lion. What new idea is gained by this title but one subversive of all credit—which the tale should force upon us—of its truth!

For me, I was never so affected with any human tale. After first reading it, I was totally possessed with it for many days. I dislike all the miraculous part of it; but the feelings of the man under the operation of such scenery, dragged me along like Tom Pipe's magic whistle. I totally differ from your idea that the *Marinere* should have had a character and profession. This is a beauty in *Gulliver's Travels*, where the mind is kept in a placid state of little wonderments; but the *Ancient Marinere* undergoes such trials as overwhelm and bury all individuality or memory of what he was—like the state of a man in a bad dream, one terrible peculiarity of which is, that all consciousness of personality is gone. Your other observation is, I think as well, a little unfounded: the 'Marinere,' from being conversant in supernatural events, *has* acquired a supernatural and strange cast of *phrase*, eye, appearance, etc., which frighten the 'wedding guest.' You will excuse my remarks, because I am hurt and vexed that you should think it necessary, with a prose apology, to open the eyes of dead men that cannot see.

To sum up a general opinion of the second volume, I do not feel any one poem in it so forcibly as the *Ancient Marinere*, and the 'Mad Mother,' and the 'Lines at Tintern Abbey' in the first.   *Letter to Wordsworth, Feb.* 1801.

COLERIDGE, *THE ANCIENT MARINER*

If you wrote that review in the *Critical Review*, I am sorry you are so sparing of praise to the *Ancient Marinere*. So far from calling it as you do, with some wit, but more severity, a

'Dutch Attempt,' etc., I call it a right English attempt, and a successful one, to dethrone German sublimity. You have selected a passage fertile in unmeaning miracles, but have passed by fifty passages as miraculous as the miracles they celebrate. I never so deeply felt the pathetic as in that part,

> A spring of love gush'd from my heart,
> And I bless'd them unaware.

It stung me into high pleasure through sufferings.

Letter to Southey, Nov. 8, 1798.

WORDSWORTH, *THE BLIND HIGHLAND BOY*

I am afraid lest that substitution of a shell (a flat falsification of the history) for the household implement, as it stood at first, was a kind of tub thrown out to the beast, or rather thrown out for him. The tub was a good honest tub in its place, and nothing could fairly be said against it. You say you made the alteration for the 'friendly reader,' but the 'malicious' will take it to himself. Damn 'em, if you give 'em an inch, etc.

Letter to Wordsworth, 1815.

REVIEW OF WORDSWORTH'S *EXCURSION*, 1814

The volume before us, as we learn from the Preface, is 'a detached portion of an unfinished poem, containing views of man, nature, and society'; to be called the Recluse, as having for its principal subject the 'sensations and opinions of a poet living in retirement'; and to be preceded by a 'record in verse of the origin and progress of the author's own powers, with reference to the fitness which they may be supposed to have conferred for the task.' To the completion of this plan we look forward with a confidence which the execution of the finished part is well calculated to inspire.—Meanwhile, in what is before us there is ample matter for entertainment: for the 'Excursion' is not a branch (as might have been suspected) prematurely plucked from the parent tree to gratify an over-hasty appetite for applause; but is, in itself, a complete and legitimate production.

It opens with the meeting of the poet with an aged man whom he had known from his school days; in plain words, a Scottish pedlar; a man who, though of low origin, had received good learning and impressions of the strictest piety from his stepfather, a minister and village schoolmaster. Among the hills of Athol, the child is described to have become familiar with the appearances of nature in his occupation as a feeder of sheep; and from her silent influences to have derived a character, meditative, tender, and poetical. With an imagination and feelings thus nourished—his intellect not unaided by books, but those, few, and chiefly of a religious cast—the necessity of seeking a maintenance in riper years, had induced him to make choice of a profession, the *appellation* for which has been gradually declining into contempt, but which formerly designated a class of men, who, journeying in country places, when roads presented less facilities for travelling, and the intercourse between towns and villages was unfrequent and hazardous, became a sort of link of neighbourhood to distant habitations; resembling, in some small measure, in the effects of their periodical returns, the caravan which Thomson so feelingly describes as blessing the cheerless Siberian in its annual visitation, with 'news of human kind.'

In the solitude incident to this rambling life, power had been given him to keep alive that devotedness to nature which he had imbibed in his childhood, together with the opportunity of gaining such notices of persons and things from his intercourse with society, as qualified him to become a 'teacher of moral wisdom.' With this man, then, in a hale old age, released from the burthen of his occupation, yet retaining much of its active habits, the poet meets, and is by him introduced to a second character—a sceptic—one who had been partially roused from an overwhelming desolation, brought upon him by the loss of wife and children, by the powerful incitement of hope which the French Revolution in its commencement put forth, but who, disgusted with the failure of all its promises, had fallen back into a laxity of faith and conduct which induced at length a total despondence as to the dignity and final destination of his species. In the language of the poet, he

> —broke faith with those whom he had laid
> In earth's dark chambers.

Yet he describes himself as subject to compunctious visitations from that silent quarter.

> —Feebly must They have felt,
> Who, in old time, attired with snakes and whips
> The vengeful Furies. *Beautiful* regards
> Were turned on me—the face of her I loved;
> The Wife and Mother; pitifully fixing
> Tender reproaches, insupportable!—p. 133.

The conversations with this person, in which the Wanderer asserts the consolatory side of the question against the darker views of human life maintained by his friend, and finally calls to his assistance the experience of a village priest, the third, or rather fourth interlocutor, (for the poet himself is one,) form the groundwork of the 'Excursion.'

It will be seen by this sketch that the poem is of a didactic nature, and not a fable or story; yet it is not wanting in stories of the most interesting kind,—such as the lovers of Cowper and Goldsmith will recognise as something familiar and congenial to them. We might instance the Ruined Cottage, and the Solitary's own story, in the first half of the work; and the second half, as being almost a continued cluster of narration. But the prevailing charm of the poem is, perhaps, that, conversational as it is in its plan, the dialogue throughout is carried on in the very heart of the most romantic scenery which the poet's native hills could supply; and which, by the perpetual references made to it either in the way of illustration or for variety and pleasurable description's sake, is brought before us as we read. We breathe in the fresh air, as we do while reading Walton's Complete Angler; only the country about us is as much bolder than Walton's, as the thoughts and speculations, which form the matter of the poem, exceed the trifling pastime and low-pitched conversation of his humble fishermen. We give the description of the 'two huge peaks,' which from some other vale peered into that in which the Solitary is entertaining the poet and companion. 'Those,' says their host,

> —if here you dwelt, would be
> Your prized Companions.—Many are the notes
> Which in his tuneful course the wind draws forth
> From rocks, woods, caverns, heaths, and dashing shores;
> And well those lofty Brethren bear their part
> In the wild concert—chiefly when the storm
> Rides high; then all the upper air they fill
> With roaring sound, that ceases not to flow,
> Like smoke, along the level of the blast
> In mighty current; theirs, too, is the song
> Of stream and headlong flood that seldom fails;

And in the grim and breathless hour of noon,
Methinks that I have heard them echo back
The thunder's greeting:—nor have Nature's laws
Left them ungifted with a power to yield
Music of finer frame; a harmony,
So do I call it, though it be the hand
Of silence, though there be no voice;—the clouds,
The mist, the shadows, light of golden suns,
Motions of moonlight, all come thither—touch,
And have an answer—thither come, and shape
A language not unwelcome to sick hearts
And idle spirits:—there the sun himself
At the calm close of summer's longest day
Rests his substantial Orb;—between those heights,
And on the top of either pinnacle,
More keenly than elsewhere in night's blue vault,
Sparkle the Stars as of their station proud.
Thoughts are not busier in the mind of man
Than the mute agent stirring there:—alone
Here do I sit and watch.—p. 84.

To a mind constituted like that of Mr Wordsworth, the stream, the torrent, and the stirring leaf—seem not merely to suggest associations of deity, but to be a kind of speaking communication with it. He walks through every forest, as through some Dodona; and every bird that flits among the leaves, like that miraculous one[1] in Tasso, but in language more intelligent, reveals to him far higher love-lays. In his poetry nothing in Nature is dead. Motion is synonymous with life. 'Beside yon spring,' says the Wanderer, speaking of a deserted well, from which, in former times, a poor woman, who died heart-broken, had been used to dispense refreshment to the thirsty traveller,

                    —beside yon Spring I stood,
And eyed its waters till we seem'd to feel
One sadness, they and I. For them a bond
Of brotherhood is broken: time has been
When, every day, the touch of human hand
Dislodged the natural sleep that binds them up
In mortal stillness;—p. 27.

To such a mind, we say—call it strength or weakness—if

---

[1] With partie coloured plumes and purple bill,
A woondrous bird among the rest there flew,
That in plaine speech sung love laies loud and shrill,
Her leden was like humaine language trew,
So much she talkt, and with such wit and skill,
That strange it seemed how much good she knew.
                              Fairefax's Translation.

weakness, assuredly a fortunate one—the visible and audible
things of creation present, not dim symbols, or curious em-
blems, which they have done at all times to those who have
been gifted with the poetical faculty; but revelations and quick
insights into the life within us, the pledge of immortality:—

> —the whispering Air
> Sends inspiration from the shadowy heights,
> And blind recesses of the caverned rocks;
> The little Rills, and Waters numberless,
> Inaudible by daylight.

'I have seen,' the poet says, and the illustration is an happy
one:

> —I have seen
> A curious Child applying to his ear
> The convolutions of a smooth-lipp'd Shell;
> To which, in silence hushed, his very soul
> Listened intensely, and his countenance soon
> Brightened with joy; for murmurings from within
> Were heard,—sonorous cadences! whereby,
> To his belief, the Monitor expressed
> Mysterious union with its native Sea.
> Even such a Shell the Universe itself
> Is to the ear of Faith; and doth impart
> Authentic tidings of invisible things;
> Of ebb and flow, and ever-during power;
> And central peace subsisting at the heart
> Of endless agitation.—p. 191.

Sometimes this harmony is imaged to us by an echo; and
in one instance, it is with such transcendant beauty set forth
by a shadow and its corresponding substance, that it would
be a sin to cheat our readers at once of so happy an illustration
of the poet's system, and so fair a proof of his descriptive
powers.

> Thus having reached a bridge, that overarched
> The hasty rivulet where it lay becalmed
> In a deep pool, by happy chance we saw
> A two-fold Image; on a grassy bank
> A snow-white Ram, and in the crystal flood
> Another and the same! Most beautiful,
> On the green turf, with his imperial front
> Shaggy and bold, and wreathed horns superb,
> The breathing Creature stood; as beautiful,
> Beneath him, showed his shadowy Counterpart.
> Each had his glowing mountains, each his sky,
> And each seemed centre of his own fair world:
> Antipodes unconscious of each other,
> Yet, in partition, with their several spheres,
> Blended in perfect stillness, to our sight!—p. 407.

Combinations, it is confessed, 'like those reflected in that quiet pool,' cannot be lasting: it is enough for the purpose of the poet, if they are felt.—They are at least his system; and his readers, if they reject them for their creed, may receive them merely as poetry. In him, *faith*, in friendly alliance and conjunction with the religion of his country, appears to have grown up, fostered by meditation and lonely communions with Nature—an internal principle of lofty consciousness, which stamps upon his opinions and sentiments (we were almost going to say) the character of an expanded and generous Quakerism.

From such a creed we should expect unusual results; and, when applied to the purposes of consolation, more touching considerations than from the mouth of common teachers. The finest speculation of this sort perhaps in the poem before us, is the notion of the thoughts which may sustain the spirit, while they crush the frame of the sufferer, who from loss of objects of love by death, is commonly supposed to pine away under a broken heart.

> —If there be whose tender frames have drooped
> Even to the dust; apparently, through weight
> Of anguish unrelieved, and lack of power
> An agonizing spirit to transmute,
> Infer not hence a hope from those withheld
> When wanted most; a confidence impaired
> So pitiably, that, having ceased to see
> With bodily eyes, they are borne down by love
> Of what is lost, and perish through regret.
> Oh! no, full oft the *innocent Sufferer sees*
> *Too clearly; feels too vividly; and longs*
> *To realize the Vision with intense*
> *And over-constant yearning*—there—there lies
> The excess, by which the balance is destroyed.
> Too, too contracted are these walls of flesh,
> This vital warmth too cold, these visual orbs,
> Though inconceivably endowed, too dim
> For any passion of the soul that leads
> To extacy; and, all the crooked paths
> Of time and change disdaining, takes its course
> Along the line of limitless desires.—p. 148.

With the same modifying and incorporating power, he tells us,—

> Within the soul a Faculty abides
> That with interpositions, which would hide
> And darken, so can deal, that they become
> Contingencies of pomp; and serve to exalt
> Her native brightness. As the ample Moon,

In the deep stillness of a summer even
Rising behind a thick and lofty Grove,
Burns like an unconsuming fire of light,
In the green trees; and, kindling on all sides
Their leafy umbrage, turns the dusky veil
Into a substance glorious as her own,
Yea with her own incorporated, by power
Capacious and serene. Like power abides
In Man's celestial Spirit; Virtue thus
Sets forth and magnifies herself; thus feeds
A calm, a beautiful, and silent fire,
From the incumbrances of mortal life,
From error, disappointment,—nay from guilt;
And sometimes, so relenting Justice wills,
From palpable oppressions of Despair.—p. 188.

This is high poetry; though (as we have ventured to lay the
basis of the author's sentiments in a sort of liberal Quakerism)
from some parts of it, others may, with more plausibility,
object to the appearance of a kind of Natural Methodism: we
could have wished therefore that the tale of Margaret had been
postponed, till the reader had been strengthened by some
previous acquaintance with the author's theory, and not placed
in the front of the poem, with a kind of ominous aspect,
beautifully tender as it is. It is a tale of a cottage, and its
female tenant, gradually decaying together, while she expected
the return of one whom poverty and not unkindness had
driven from her arms. We trust ourselves only with the con-
clusion—
                              Nine tedious years;
From their first separation, nine long years,
She lingered in unquiet widowhood,
A Wife and Widow. I have heard, my Friend,
That in yon arbour oftentimes she sate
Alone, through half the vacant Sabbath-day;
And, if a dog passed by, she still would quit
The shade, and look abroad. On this old Bench
For hours she sate; and evermore her eye
Was busy in the distance, shaping things
That made her heart beat quick. You see that path;
There, to and fro, she paced through many a day
Of the warm summer, from a belt of hemp
That girt her waist, spinning the long-drawn thread
With backward steps. Yet ever as there pass'd
A man whose garments shew'd the Soldier's red[1],
The little child who sate to turn the wheel,
Ceas'd from his task; and she with faultering voice
Made many a fond enquiry; and when they,

---

[1] Her husband had enlisted for a soldier.

Whose presence gave no comfort, were gone by,
Her heart was still more sad. And by yon gate,
That bars the Traveller's road, she often stood,
And, when a stranger Horseman came, the latch
Would lift, and in his face look wistfully;
Most happy, if, from aught discovered there
Of tender feeling, she might dare repeat
The same sad question. Meanwhile her poor Hut
Sank to decay: for he was gone—whose hand,
At the first nipping of October frost,
Closed up each chink, and with fresh bands of straw
Checquered the green-grown thatch. And so she lived
Through the long winter, reckless and alone;
Until her home by frost, and thaw, and rain,
Was sapped; and while she slept the nightly damps
Did chill her breast; and in the stormy day
Her tattered clothes were ruffled by the wind;
Even at the side of her own fire. Yet still
She loved this wretched spot, nor would for worlds
Have parted hence: and still that length of road,
And this rude bench, one torturing hope endeared,
Fast rooted at her heart: and here, my Friend,
In sickness she remained; and here she died,
Last human Tenant of these ruined Walls.—p. 44.

The fourth book, entitled 'Despondency Corrected,' we consider as the most valuable portion of the poem. For moral
grandeur; for wide scope of thought and a long train of lofty
imagery; for tender personal appeals; and a *versification* which
we feel we ought to notice, but feel it also so involved in the
poetry, that we can hardly mention it as a distinct excellence; it
stands without competition among our didactic and descriptive
verse. The general tendency of the argument (which we might
almost affirm to be the leading moral of the poem) is to abate
the pride of the calculating *understanding*, and to reinstate the
imagination and the *affections* in those seats from which modern
philosophy has laboured but too successfully to expel them.
'Life's autumn past,' says the grey-haired Wanderer,

—I stand on Winter's verge,
And daily lose what I desire to keep:
Yet rather would I instantly decline
To the traditionary sympathies
Of a most rustic ignorance, and take
A fearful apprehension from the owl
Or death-watch,—and as readily rejoice,
If two auspicious magpies crossed my way;
This rather would I do than see and hear
The repetitions wearisome of sense,
Where soul is dead, and feeling hath no place;—p. 168.

7—2

In the same spirit, those illusions of the imaginative faculty to which the peasantry in solitary districts are peculiarly subject, are represented as the kindly ministers of *conscience*:

> —with whose service charged
> They come and go, appear and disappear;
> Diverting evil purposes, remorse
> Awakening, chastening an intemperate grief,
> Or pride of heart abating.

Reverting to more distant ages of the world, the operation of that same faculty in producing the several fictions of Chaldean, Persian, and Grecian idolatry, is described with such seductive power, that the Solitary, in good earnest, seems alarmed at the tendency of his own argument.— Notwithstanding his fears, however, there is one thought so uncommonly fine, relative to the spirituality which lay hid beneath the gross material forms of Greek worship, in metal or stone, that we cannot resist the allurement of transcribing it—

> —triumphant o'er this pompous show
> Of Art, this palpable array of Sense,
> On every side encountered; in despite
> Of the gross fictions, chaunted in the streets
> By wandering Rhapsodists; and in contempt
> Of doubt and bold denials hourly urged
> Amid the wrangling Schools—a SPIRIT hung,
> Beautiful Region! o'er thy Towns and Farms,
> Statues and Temples, and memorial Tombs;
> And emanations were perceived; and acts
> Of immortality, in Nature's course,
> Exemplified by mysteries, that were felt
> As bonds, on grave Philosopher imposed
> And armed Warrior; and in every grove
> A gay or pensive tenderness prevailed,
> When piety more awful had relaxed.
>   'Take, running River, take these Locks of mine'—
> Thus would the Votary say—'this severed hair,
> My Vow fulfilling, do I here present,
> Thankful for my beloved Child's return.
> Thy banks, Cephissus, he again hath trod,
> Thy murmurs heard; and drunk the chrystal lymph
> With which thou dost refresh the thirsty lip,
> And moisten all day long these flowery fields.'
> And doubtless, sometimes, when the hair was shed
> Upon the flowing stream, a thought arose
> Of Life continuous, Being unimpaired;

That hath been, is, and where it was and is
There shall be,—seen, and heard, and felt, and known,
And recognized,—existence unexposed
To the blind walk of mortal accident;
From diminution safe and weakening age;
While Man grows old, and dwindles, and decays;
And countless generations of Mankind
Depart; and leave no vestige where they trod.—p. 173.

In discourse like this the first day passes away. The second
(for this almost dramatic poem takes up the action of two
summer days) is varied by the introduction of the village
priest; to whom the Wanderer resigns the office of chief
speaker, which had been yielded to his age and experience on
the first. The conference is begun at the gate of the church-yard;
and after some natural speculations concerning death and immortality—and the custom of funereal and sepulchral obser-
vances, as deduced from a feeling of immortality—certain doubts
are proposed respecting the quantity of moral worth existing
in the world, and in the mountainous district in particular. In
the resolution of these doubts, the priest enters upon a most
affecting and singular strain of narration, derived from the
graves around him. Pointing to hillock after hillock, he gives
short histories of their tenants, disclosing their humble virtues,
and touching with tender hand upon their frailties.

Nothing can be conceived finer than the manner of intro-
ducing these tales. With heaven above his head, and the
mouldering turf at his feet—standing betwixt life and death—
he seems to maintain that spiritual relation which he bore to
his living flock, in its undiminished strength, even with their
ashes; and to be in his proper cure, or diocese, among the dead.

We might extract powerful instances of pathos from these
tales—the story of Ellen in particular—but their force is in
combination, and in the circumstances under which they are
introduced. The traditionary anecdote of the Jacobite and
Hanoverian, as less liable to suffer by transplanting, and as
affording an instance of that finer species of humour, that
thoughtful playfulness in which the author more nearly perhaps
than in any other quality resembles Cowper, we shall lay (at
least a part of it) before our readers. It is the story of a whig
who, having wasted a large estate in election contests, retired
'beneath a borrowed name' to a small town among these
northern mountains, where a Caledonian laird, a follower of
the house of Stuart, who had fled his country after the over-

throw at Culloden, returning with the return of lenient times,
had also fixed his residence.

                    —Here, then, they met,
Two doughty Champions; flaming Jacobite
And sullen Hanoverian! you might think
That losses and vexations, less severe
Than those which they had severally sustained,
Would have inclined each to abate his zeal
For his ungrateful cause; no,—I have heard
My reverend Father tell that, mid the calm
Of that small Town encountering thus, they filled,
Daily, its Bowling-green with harmless strife;
Plagued with uncharitable thoughts the Church;
And vexed the Market-place. But in the breasts
Of these Opponents gradually was wrought,
With little change of general sentiment,
Such change towards each other, that their days
By choice were spent in constant fellowship;
And if, at times, they fretted with the yoke,
Those very bickerings made them love it more.

    A favourite boundary to their lengthened walks
This Church-yard was. And, whether they had come
Treading their path in sympathy and linked
In social converse, or by some short space
Discreetly parted to preserve the peace,
One Spirit seldom failed to extend its sway
Over both minds, when they awhile had marked
The visible quiet of this holy ground
And breathed its soothing air;—
                    [*Seven lines omitted.*]
—There live who yet remember to have seen
Their courtly Figures,—seated on a stump
Of an old Yew, their favourite resting-place.
But, as the Remnant of the long-lived Tree
Was disappearing by a swift decay,
They, with joint care, determined to erect,
Upon its site, a Dial, which should stand
For public use; and also might survive
As their own private monument; for this
Was the particular spot, in which they wished
(And Heaven was pleased to accomplish their desire)
That, undivided, their Remains should lie.
So, where the mouldered Tree had stood, was raised
Yon Structure, framing, with the ascent of steps
That to the decorated Pillar lead,
A work of art, more sumptuous, as might seem,
Than suits this Place; yet built in no proud scorn
Of rustic homeliness; they only aimed
To ensure for it respectful guardianship.
Around the margin of the Plate, whereon
The Shadow falls, to note the stealthy hours,

Winds an inscriptive Legend,——At these words
Thither we turned; and gathered, as we read,
The appropriate sense, in Latin numbers couched.
'Time flies; it is his melancholy task
To bring, and bear away, delusive hopes,
And re-produce the troubles he destroys.
But, while his blindness thus is occupied,
Discerning Mortal! do thou serve the will
Of Time's eternal Master, and that peace,
Which the World wants, shall be for Thee confirmed.'
—pp. 270-3.

The causes which have prevented the poetry of Mr Wordsworth from attaining its full share of popularity are to be found
in the boldness and originality of his genius. The times are
past when a poet could securely follow the direction of his
own mind into whatever tracts it might lead. A writer, who
would be popular, must timidly coast the shore of prescribed
sentiment and sympathy. He must have just as much more of
the imaginative faculty than his readers, as will serve to keep
their apprehensions from stagnating, but not so much as to
alarm their jealousy. He must not think or feel too deeply.

If he has had the fortune to be bred in the midst of the most
magnificent objects of creation, he must not have given away
his heart to them; or if he have, he must conceal his love, or
not carry his expressions of it beyond that point of rapture,
which the occasional tourist thinks it not overstepping decorum to betray, or the limit which that gentlemanly spy upon
Nature, the picturesque traveller, has vouchsafed to countenance.
He must do this, or be content to be thought an enthusiast.

If from living among simple mountaineers, from a daily
intercourse with them, not upon the footing of a patron, but
in the character of an equal, he has detected, or imagines that
he has detected, through the cloudy medium of their unlettered
discourse, thoughts and apprehensions not vulgar; traits of
patience and constancy, love unwearied and heroic endurance,
not unfit (as he may judge) to be made the subject of verse, he
will be deemed a man of perverted genius by the philanthropist
who, conceiving of the peasantry of his country only as objects
of a pecuniary sympathy, starts at finding them elevated to a
level of humanity with himself, having their own loves, enmities, cravings, aspirations, etc., as much beyond his faculty
to believe, as his beneficence to supply.

If from a familiar observation of the ways of children, and
much more from a retrospect of his own mind when a child,

he has gathered more reverential notions of that state than fall
to the lot of ordinary observers, and, escaping from the dissonant wranglings of men, has tuned his lyre, though but for
occasional harmonies, to the milder utterance of that soft age,
—his verses shall be censured as infantile by critics who confound poetry 'having children for its subject' with poetry
that is 'childish,' and who, having themselves perhaps never
been *children*, never having possessed the tenderness and
docility of that age, know not what the soul of a child is—how
apprehensive! how imaginative! how religious!

We have touched upon some of the causes which we conceive to have been unfriendly to the author's former poems.
We think they do not apply in the same force to the one before
us. There is in it more of uniform elevation, a wider scope of
subject, less of manner, and it contains none of those starts
and imperfect shapings which in some of this author's smaller
pieces offended the weak, and gave scandal to the perverse.
It must indeed be approached with seriousness. It has in it
much of that quality which 'draws the devout, deterring the
profane.' Those who hate the Paradise Lost will not love this
poem. The steps of the great master are discernible in it; not
in direct imitation or injurious parody, but in the following of
the spirit, in free homage and generous subjection.

One objection it is impossible not to foresee. It will be
asked, why put such eloquent discourse in the mouth of a
pedlar? It might be answered that Mr Wordsworth's plan
required a character in humble life to be the organ of his
philosophy. It was in harmony with the system and scenery
of his poem. We read Piers Plowman's Creed, and the lowness
of the teacher seems to add a simple dignity to the doctrine.
Besides, the poet has bestowed an unusual share of education
upon him. Is it too much to suppose that the author, at some
early period of his life, may himself have known such a person,
a man endowed with sentiments above his situation, another
Burns; and that the dignified strains which he has attributed
to the Wanderer may be no more than recollections of his
conversation, heightened only by the amplification natural to
poetry, or the lustre which imagination flings back upon the
objects and companions of our youth? After all, if there should
be found readers willing to admire the poem, who yet feel
scandalized at a *name*, we would advise them, wherever it
occurs, to substitute silently the word *Palmer*, or *Pilgrim*, or

any less offensive designation, which shall connect the notion of sobriety in heart and manners with the experience and privileges which a wayfaring life confers.

The Quarterly Review. 1814.

CHARLES LAMB

There is an order of imperfect intellects (under which mine must be content to rank) which in its constitution is essentially anti-Caledonian. The owners of the sort of faculties I allude to, have minds rather suggestive than comprehensive. They have no pretences to much clearness or precision in their ideas, or in their manner of expressing them. Their intellectual wardrobe (to confess fairly) has few whole pieces in it. They are content with fragments and scattered pieces of Truth. She presents no full front to them—a feature or side-face at the most. Hints and glimpses, germs and crude essays at a system, is the utmost they pretend to. They beat up a little game per-adventure—and leave it to knottier heads, more robust con-stitutions, to run it down. The light that lights them is not steady and polar, but mutable and shifting: waxing, and again waning. Their conversation is accordingly. They will throw out a random word in or out of season, and be content to let it pass for what it is worth. They cannot speak always as if they were upon their oath—but must be understood, speaking or writing, with some abatement. They seldom wait to mature a proposition, but e'en bring it to market in the green ear. They delight to impart their defective discoveries as they arise, without waiting for their full developement. They are no systematizers, and would but err more by attempting it. Their minds, as I said before, are suggestive merely.

Imperfect Sympathies, in *The Essays of Elia.* 1821.

CHARLES LAMB, *THE ESSAYS OF ELIA*

Crude they are, I grant you—a sort of unlicked, incondite things—villainously pranked in an affected array of antique modes and phrases. They had not been *his*, if they had been other than such; and better it is, that a writer should be natural in a self-pleasing quaintness, than to affect a naturalness (so called) that should be strange to him.

Preface to The Last Essays of Elia. 1823.

BYRON

I never can make out his great *power*, which his admirers talk of. Why, a line of Wordsworth's is a lever to lift the immortal spirit! Byrons can only move the Spleen. He was at best a Satyrist—in any other way he was mean enough.

Letter to Barton, May, 1824.

SHELLEY

I can no more understand Shelley than you can. His poetry is 'thin sown with profit or delight.' Yet I must point to your notice a sonnet conceiv'd and expressed with a witty delicacy. It is that addressed to one who hated him, but who could not persuade him to hate *him* again. His coyness to the other's passion (for hate demands a return as much as Love, and starves without it) is most arch and pleasant. Pray, like it very much.

For his theories and nostrums, they are oracular enough, but I either comprehend 'em not, or there is miching malice and mischief in 'em. But, for the most part, ringing with their own emptiness. Hazlitt said well of 'em—Many are the wiser and better for reading Shakspeare, but nobody was ever wiser or better for reading Shelley.

Letter to Barton, Aug. 1824.

JOHN CLARE

I am an inveterate old Londoner, but while I am among your choice collections I seem to be native to them and free of the country. The quantity of your observation has astonished me. What have most pleased me have been 'Recollections after a Ramble,' and those 'Grongar Hill' kind of pieces in eight-syllable lines, my favourite measure, such as 'Cowper Hill' and 'Solitude.' In some of your story-telling ballads the provincial phrases sometimes startle me. I think you are too profuse with them. In poetry, *slang* of every kind is to be avoided. There is a rustic Cockneyism as little pleasing as ours of London. Transplant Arcadia to Helpstone. The true rustic style, the Arcadian English, I think is to be found in Shenstone. Would his 'Schoolmistress,' the prettiest of poems, have been

better if he had used quite the Goody's own language? Now
and then a home rusticism is fresh and startling, but where
nothing is gained in expression it is out of tenor. It may make
folks smile and stare, but the ungenial coalition of barbarous
with refined phrases will prevent you in the end from being
so generally tasted as you deserve to be.

Letter to John Clare, Aug. 31, 1822.

REVIEW OF KEATS' *LAMIA*

LAMIA, ISABELLA, THE EVE OF SAINT AGNES, AND OTHER POEMS. BY JOHN KEATS. AUTHOR OF *ENDYMION*

A casement high and triple-arch'd there was,
All garlanded with carven imag'ries
Of fruits, and flowers, and bunches of knot-grass,
And diamonded with panes of quaint device,
Innumerable of stains and splendid dyes,
As are the tiger-moth's deep-damask'd wings;
And in the midst, 'mong thousand heraldries,
And twilight saints, and dim emblazonings,
A shielded 'scutcheon blush'd with blood of Queens and Kings.

Full on this casement shone the wintry moon,
And threw warm gules on Madeline's fair breast,
As down she knelt for Heaven's grace and boon;
Rose-bloom fell on her hands, together prest,
And on her silver cross soft amethyst,
And on her hair a glory, like a saint:
She seem'd a splendid angel, newly drest,
Save wings, for Heaven——

                              Her vespers done,
Of all its wreathed pearls her hair she frees,
Unclasps her warmed jewels one by one;
Loosens her fragrant boddice; by degrees
Her rich attire creeps rustling to her knees;
Half-hidden, like a mermaid in sea-weed,
Pensive awhile she dreams awake, and sees,
In fancy, fair Saint Agnes in her bed,
But dares not look behind, or all the charm is fled.

Soon, trembling in her soft and chilly nest,
In sort of wakeful swoon, perplex'd she lay,
Until the poppied warmth of sleep oppress'd
Her soothed limbs, and soul fatigued away;
Flown, like a thought, until the morrow-day;
Blissfully haven'd both from joy and pain;
Clasp'd like a missal where swart Paynims pray;
Blinded alike from sunshine and from rain,
As though a rose should shut, and be a bud again.

Such is the description which Mr Keats has given us, with
a delicacy worthy of Christabel, of a high-born damsel, in one
of the apartments of a baronial castle, laying herself down
devoutly to dream, on the charmed Eve of St Agnes; and like
the radiance, which comes from those old windows upon the
limbs and garments of the damsel, is the almost Chaucer-like
painting, with which this poet illumes every subject he touches.
We have scarcely anything like it in modern description. It
brings us back to ancient days, and

> Beauty making-beautiful old rhymes.

The finest thing in the volume is the paraphrase of Boccaccio's story of the Pot of Basil. Two Florentines, merchants,
discovering that their sister Isabella has placed her affections
upon Lorenzo, a young factor in their employ, when they had
hopes of procuring for her a noble match, decoy Lorenzo,
under the pretence of a ride, into a wood, where they suddenly
stab and bury him. The anticipation of the assassination is
wonderfully conceived in one epithet, in the narration of the
ride—

> So the two brothers, and their *murder'd* man,
>   Rode past fair Florence, to where Arno's stream
> Gurgles——

Returning to their sister, they delude her with a story of their
having sent Lorenzo abroad to look after their merchandises;
but the spirit of her lover appears to Isabella in a dream, and
discovers how and where he was stabbed, and the spot where
they have buried him. To ascertain the truth of the vision,
she sets out to the place, accompanied by her old nurse,
ignorant as yet of her wild purpose. Her arrival at it, and
digging for the body, is described in the following stanzas,
than which there is nothing more awfully simple in diction,
more nakedly grand and moving in sentiment, in Dante, in
Chaucer, or in Spenser:—

> She gaz'd into the fresh-thrown mould, as though
>   One glance did fully all its secrets tell;
> Clearly she saw, as other eyes would know
>   Pale limbs at bottom of a crystal well;
> Upon the murderous spot she seem'd to grow,
>   Like to a native lily of the dell:
> Then with her knife, all sudden, she began
> To dig more fervently than misers can.

Soon she turn'd up a soiled glove, whereon
　　Her silk had play'd in purple phantasies,
She kissed it with a lip more chill than stone,
　　And put it in her bosom, where it dries
And freezes utterly unto the bone
　　Those dainties made to still an infant's cries:
Then 'gan she work again; nor stay'd her care,
But to throw back at times her veiling hair.

That old nurse stood beside her wondering,
　　Until her heart felt pity to the core
At sight of such a dismal labouring,
　　And so she kneeled, with her locks all hoar,
And put her lean hand to the horrid thing:
　　Three hours they labour'd at this travail sore;
At last they felt the kernel of the grave,
And Isabella did not stamp and rave.

To pursue the story in prose:—They find the body, and
with their joint strengths sever from it the head, which Isabella
takes home, and wrapping it in a silken scarf, entombs it in
her garden-pot, covers it with mould, and over it she plants
sweet basil, which, watered with her tears, thrives so that no
other basil tufts in all Florence throve like her basil. How her
brothers, suspecting something mysterious in this herb, which
she watched day and night, at length discover the head, and
secretly convey the basil from her; and how from the day that
she loses her basil she pines away, and at last dies, we must
refer our reader to the poem, or to the divine germ of it in
Boccaccio. It is a great while ago since we read the original;
and in this affecting revival of it we do but

Weep again a long-forgotten woe.

More exuberantly rich in imagery and painting is the story
of the Lamia. It is of as gorgeous stuff as ever romance was
composed of. Her first appearance in serpentine form—

—a beauteous wreath with melancholy eyes—

her dialogue with Hermes, the *Star of Lethe*, as he is called by
one of these prodigal phrases which Mr Keats abounds in,
which are each a poem in a word, and which in this instance
lays open to us at once, like a picture, all the dim regions and
their inhabitants, and the sudden coming of a celestial among
them; the charming of her into woman's shape again by the
God; her marriage with the beautiful Lycius; her magic
palace, which those who knew the street, and remembered it

complete from childhood, never remembered to have seen
before; the few Persian mutes, her attendants,

> —who that same year
> Were seen about the markets: none knew where
> They could inhabit;—

the high-wrought splendours of the nuptial bower, with the
fading of the whole pageantry, Lamia, and all, away, before
the glance of Apollonius,—are all that fairy land can do for
us. They are for younger impressibilities. To *us* an ounce of
feeling is worth a pound of fancy; and therefore we recur
again, with a warmer gratitude, to the story of Isabella and the
pot of basil, and those never-cloying stanzas which we have
cited, and which we think should disarm criticism, if it be not
in its nature cruel; if it would not deny to honey its sweetness,
nor to roses redness, nor light to the stars in Heaven; if it
would not bay the moon out of the skies, rather than acknowledge she is fair.

The New Times. 1820.

NOTES

p. 2, l. 34, "Tyke." A character in Thomas Morton's *School of Reform*, 1805.

p. 5, l. 31, "Withers." A mistake for "Wither."

p. 5, l. 35, "a happier genius." Presumably Scott.

p. 7, l. 4. There is doubt about the date of Lamb's letter to Elton. See E. V. Lucas, *Works of Charles and Mary Lamb*, VII, p. 651.

p. 7, l. 31, "a later Sydney." Algernon Sidney, who, though an officer in the Parliamentary army, refused to take part in the proceedings that ended with the execution of Charles I.

p. 13, l. 32, "W. H." William Hazlitt, who in his *Lectures on the Age of Elizabeth*, lecture VI (see Waller and Glover, *Collected Works of William Hazlitt*, v, pp. 318–326) speaks slightingly of *Arcadia* and calls the *Sonnets* "jejune, far-fetched and frigid."

p. 15, l. 8, "Characters of Dramatic Writers Contemporary with Shakspeare." In 1808 Lamb published an anthology of the Elizabethan drama entitled *Specimens of Dramatic Poets who lived about the Time of Shakspeare*. To most of these extracts he added notes. It is these notes, collected and revised, that form the text of his *Characters of Dramatic Writers Contemporary with Shakspeare*, published in the *Works* of 1818.

p. 16, l. 4, "Lust's Dominion." It has been found that this play was not written by Marlowe.

p. 16, l. 15, "a pleasant burlesque of mine ancient's." See Pistol in *Henry IV, Part 2*, II, 4, 177–181.

p. 19, l. 28, "the author of God's Revenge against Murder." John Reynolds, whose writings fall between the years 1620 and 1640.

p. 26, l. 37, "Guzman, in that excellent old translation of the Spanish Rogue." Lamb is referring to Mateo Aleman's romance *Guzman de Alfarache*, published in 1599 and 1605. Mr E. V. Lucas, *Works of Charles and Mary Lamb*, II, p. 449, says that Lamb had a copy of the English translation (1622) by James Mabbe entitled *The Rogue*.

p. 30, l. 6, "Donne has a copy of verses to his mistress." Lamb refers to Donne's 16th Elegy *On his Mistress* (Grierson's edition of Donne's poems, I, p. 111).

p. 36, ll. 6 and 7, "Mr K." and "Mrs S." Kemble and Mrs Siddons.

p. 44, l. 7, "Mr C." G. F. Cooke. See pp. 51–3.

p. 44, l. 39, "Glenalvon." A character in Home's *Douglas*.

p. 51, l. 34, "this Actor" refers to G. F. Cooke mentioned immediately after.

p. 61, l. 21, "the Author of 'Guzman de Alfarache.'" See note on p. 26, l. 37.

p. 72, l. 20, "Willy himself." Presumably Shakespeare.

p. 85, l. 35, "'divine chit-chat of Cowper.'" Lamb quotes Coleridge's own phrase.

p. 91, l. 3, "St Leon," a novel by Godwin.

p. 92, l. 11, "substitution of a shell for the household implement." In the original draft of the poem the blind Highland boy launched a wash-tub for his journey. Wordsworth later substituted a large shell for the wash-tub.

p. 92, l. 19, "Review of Wordsworth's *Excursion*." Lamb in a letter to Wordsworth of December 1814 tells how Gifford mutilated his review before inserting it in the *Quarterly*. "Every pretty expression (I know there were many), every warm expression (there was nothing else), is vulgarised and frozen." Lamb's original has not survived: we have only the *Quarterly* version.

p. 106, l. 10, "a sonnet." This refers not to a sonnet but to thirteen *Lines to a Reviewer* beginning,

> Alas, good friend, what profit can you see
> In hating such a hateless thing as me?

INDEX